Central Issues
in Jurisprudence

AUSTRALIA
The Law Book Company
Sydney

CANADA
The Carswell Company
Toronto, Ontario

INDIA
N. M. Tripathi (Private) Ltd.
Bombay
and
Eastern Law House (Private) Ltd.
Calcutta
M.P.P. House
Bangalore
Universal Book Traders
Delhi

ISRAEL
Steimatzky's Agency Ltd.
Tel-Aviv

PAKISTAN
Pakistan Law House
Karachi

Central Issues in Jurisprudence

Justice, Law and Rights

by

N. E. SIMMONDS, M.A., LL.M.

Fellow of Corpus Christi College
Lecturer in Law in the University of Cambridge

LONDON
SWEET & MAXWELL
1986

Published in 1986 by
Sweet & Maxwell Limited of
South Quay Plaza,
183 Marsh Wall, London E14 9FT
Set by Burgess and Son (Abingdon) Limited
Printed and bound in Great Britain by
Butler & Tanner Ltd, Frome and London

Second impression 1987
Third impression 1990
Fourth impression 1992
Fifth impression 1994

British Library Cataloguing in Publication Data

Simmonds, N.E.
    Central issues in jurisprudence: justice,
    law and rights.
    1. Jurisprudence
    I. Title
    340'.1   K230

    ISBN 0-421-35110-1
    ISBN 0-421-35120-9 Pbk

Preface

In this book, I have tried to do a straightforward job in a workmanlike fashion. Studying jurisprudence is a matter of reading books by such authors as Rawls, Nozick, Hart and Dworkin. It is not, or should not be, a matter of ploughing through a textbook that tells you *about* these books. Nevertheless, a student needs some preliminary orientation. He needs to know what the major theories under discussion are, and approximately how they relate to each other. Only someone who can't remember what it is like to *be* a student can imagine that a sketch-map of some sort is unnecessary.

One type of introductory book on jurisprudence tries to describe the key problems without much exposition of rival theories. The author tries to give the student a feel for the basic dilemmas of jurisprudence without descending to the "Hart says this, and Dworkin says that" level. Such books face insuperable difficulties, for it is not possible to produce a neutral account of the problems of jurisprudence around which the various theories can later be assembled. Hart, Dworkin and Fuller (for example) do not differ from each other simply in the answers they offer to a shared question: they differ also in their conception of what the basic questions are. In this respect jurisprudence shares a basic characteristic with other philosophical inquiries: it is self-reflective, in that its questions include questions about its own nature and status as a subject. The "problem-based" approach (if I may so style it) to jurisprudence thus misfires. Instead of studying the views of Hart, Dworkin, Rawls *et al.*, the student winds up trying to fit their theories into the framework established by the author of the introductory text; and, if the book really is of an *introductory* nature, the framework it develops is unlikely to be a very profound or revealing one.

The other defect with the "problem-based" type of introduction is this. The student (let us say) absorbs the framework offered by his introductory text. He then begins to study Rawls. Even if we assume (what is by no means certain) that Rawls can and should be fitted into the framework, where should he be fitted? Only after the student has understood Rawls can he answer the question. In other words, the introductory framework can only be applied when it is no longer of any use.

The introductory text that I have written adopts an approach that is more conventional, less ambitious, but ultimately more useful. It is a sketch-map, telling the student roughly who says what and how one thing relates to another. It gives him the basic geography of the subject. This approach requires that the author should have strong opinions about what goes onto the map: otherwise the map will become so cluttered that it is no less complex than the reality it seeks to sketch. But in representing the way in which one feature relates to another, the author should let his own opinions take a back seat. After all, the whole point is to avoid imposing on the original texts (Hart, Dworkin, *etc., etc.*) a framework of thought that may be interesting but is alien to the texts themselves. Therefore, I do not make the conventional claim that the book is chiefly for beginners but will not be without interest for experts. The book will and should be utterly without interest for experts. It wasn't written for *them*!

If this book is a sketch-map it is most certainly not a guide book. I do not claim to point out all the interesting features that will be found along the way (it's more fun to discover them for yourself!). I describe only a few major landmarks and principal highways: just enough to get you started.

To some teachers of jurisprudence, the choice of topics covered may seem unusually narrow. Where are the discussions of sociological jurisprudence and the historical school that we expect to find in textbooks of jurisprudence? Why the heavy emphasis on political theory, and *liberal* political theory at that?

I have kept the focus of the book narrow because that is the only way of enabling students to grapple with the original texts. A student who, by the end of the year, has read Rawls, Nozick, Hart and Dworkin will understand a considerable amount of jurisprudence. A student who knows the labels and potted summaries of two dozen different theories knows nothing of value. In choosing to focus on the political theory side of jurisprudence, I am nailing my flag to the mast. As I have tried to argue in my book *The Decline of Juridical Reason* (Manchester University Press 1984), the classic disputes of jurisprudence (and, indeed, "sociological" approaches such as that of Roscoe Pound) derive their significance from deep antinomies within the legal order. At the present day, one key issue concerns the relationship between a rights-based model of private law doctrine, and a revisionist attempt to place the whole law on a public and instrumentalist footing. Such crises can be comprehended only in the context of modern liberalism and its problematic self-understanding. If this approach is criticised as narrow, it should be remembered that such narrowness can be avoided only at the price of vacuity.

One omission may attract particular criticism: I have included no discussion of Marxist theories of law, or Marxist critiques of justice. This is simply because such theories could not have been intelligently explained and discussed without at least doubling the book's length and altering its whole character. A single chapter on the subject could be no more than a crude distortion. Indeed, there is a sense in which this book derives its central focus and rationale from a concern to understand the nature of liberalism. We must attempt to understand the place of law and justice within the structure of liberal thought, and we must subject the values of liberalism to careful scrutiny so as to reveal their coherence, or to expose their lack of it. This task is a necessary preliminary to any evaluation of the Marxist critique. The exposition and evaluation of that critique is a separate task, and one best left to another occasion.

N. E. SIMMONDS
Corpus Christi College,
Cambridge

ALSO BY N. E. SIMMONDS

THE DECLINE OF JURIDICAL REASON
(MANCHESTER UNIVERSITY PRESS, 1984)

Contents

Introduction: Studying Jurisprudence

The majority of law students coming to jurisprudence for the first time have in their minds a more or less definite picture of law and of legal studies. They think of law as a body of rules laid down by legislatures and by judges. The central task of the law student, they imagine, is to learn the rules and also to master various skills or techniques of arguing with rules. Sometimes there are special courses that purport to explain these techniques. More commonly, the students just have to pick up the techniques as they go along, studying contract, tort and property. The more enlightened students will also feel that it is important to reflect upon and criticise the law from a moral perspective. They will want to ask questions about the policies that the legal rules serve: are the policies the right ones, and how effectively do the rules implement them? The fact that these latter questions are rarely discussed in any very rigorous or systematic way by the books they read and the teachers they listen to does not worry the students unduly. After all, the main thing is to learn *the law*, and that means the black letter rules.

These ideas of law and legal study are shaped by a great many diverse influences. The fact that most law teachers share the assumptions and allow them to form the taken for granted basis of their courses is, perhaps, only a minor contributory factor, though nevertheless a real one. The special difficulty for the jurisprudence teacher lies in the fact that student attitudes towards jurisprudence are themselves shaped by the background assumptions. Yet it is precisely those assumptions that the jurisprudence teacher will wish to challenge. Even if he ultimately endorses the black letter view of law, the jurisprudence teacher will want the students to see it as something challengeable, controversial, and forming a part of a much wider philosophical or ideological standpoint.

In this way the jurisprudence teacher is bound to find himself at loggerheads with his colleagues. For, in teaching a substantive law subject, they must of necessity employ *some* conception of law. The healthiest situation is perhaps where different teachers hold different conceptions. But this is not usually the case, and in most Law Faculties the situation will be that the black letter view is the basis of teaching in the substantive law subjects, while the jurisprudence teacher snipes at it from the sidelines.

The best way of enforcing a particular view of things is to simply take it for granted. A view of law as a body of ascertainable rules established to serve social policies is taken for granted by most law teachers, and is therefore accepted as unquestionable by most students. Because that conception of law is *unquestionable*, the student assumes that no sane person will question it. It follows that *if* jurisprudence is a respectable discipline, it must be *consistent* with the unquestionable view of law that has been endorsed in all the other subjects of the law course. The student's understanding of what jurisprudence is about must then be fitted in to the accepted view of law. Some students will expect jurisprudence to be the long awaited systematic discussion of policy issues that, in the classes on substantive law, always seemed to be just around the corner yet never quite arrived. Others will vaguely assume that jurisprudence is about "how the legal system works" or about "what judges do", or they will just conclude that it is a lot of waffle about nothing.

The best way of beginning the study of jurisprudence is, therefore, to attack the conception of law that is so firmly rooted in the students' minds. This is not to say that that conception of law is *wrong* and must be eradicated: it may well be that in the end we will agree with the assumptions that characterised our pre-philosophical thinking. But the *first* aim must be to get the student worried, to make him see that there are problems with his taken for granted assumptions, puzzles that are hard to resolve and that lead into surprisingly deep intellectual waters. The *ultimate* aim must be to make the student aware that whatever conception of law he ultimately endorses will not be a straightforward reflection of given facts, but an element in a complex and far reaching philosophical position.

The black letter view of law assumes that we can establish what the existing law is without much difficulty. It is true that part of the law student's task is to learn how one discovers what the law is. But the problems at this level are merely ones of finding your way around the law library and the reference books. The skills of legal research are thought of as the ability to discover which rules have been authoritatively laid down in statutes and decided cases. But if the law consists of rules which have been positively established and which can be ascertained without difficulty, how does it come about that expert lawyers frequently disagree? Rival Q.C.s or law professors may disagree about what the existing law *is*. Many appellate decisions adjudicate between rival views of the existing law. But how can this be if the law is so unproblematic? When Professor X and Professor Y disagree about the law of tort, does that show that one of them has not done his homework, and has overlooked some statute or case that the other one has discovered? But we know that in most such disputes all the statutes and cases are, as it were, on the table and known to both parties. So why can they not just *see* what the rules are?

If we focus our attention on legal arguments conducted in court we might be tempted by the following explanation. The advocates *purport* to disagree about what the law is, but are in fact attempting to persuade the court to decide the case this way or that by establishing a *new* rule. Their arguments, although dressed up as legal arguments, are in fact policy arguments concerned with how the law ought to be changed. To extend this interpretation to academic disputes we would need to say that when Professor X's book on tort disagrees with Professor Y's book, this can only be because they are presenting policy arguments about what the law *ought* to be in the guise of legal arguments about what it *is*. In so far as they genuinely restricted themselves to stating the law as it is, there could be no room for dispute between them (provided that both are minimally competent in the business of discovering relevant rules).

But this explanation will not do. For, if law really is a body of positive black letter rules, how could anyone "dress up" a policy argument as a legal argument? How could anyone present policy considerations in the guise of legal reasoning? If law is all black letter rules, then legal argument is simply a matter of invoking black letter rules. If there is no room for disagreement in this view of law there is, equally, no room for *pretence*.

Let us now consider how case law fits in to this idea of law as positively established rules. Presumably we must think of decided cases as laying down rules. We know that the rule is a legal rule because it was laid down by a judge. Of course, we also know that judges do not always expressly formulate the rule on which the case is decided; and even if they do expressly formulate a rule we need not regard their formulation as decisive. In each case we must establish what the *ratio decidendi* of the case was, and to do this we must scrutinise the facts of the case and the details of the judgment.

(This mysterious process of ascertaining the *ratio* of a case helps to explain how there can be disagreement about what the law actually says; but does it not also cast doubt on the idea that the law consists of established rules?) Now suppose that we have ascertained the ratio of a case. We have reached a definite account of the rule established by the case (that such an account is possible is assumed by the conception of law that we are examining). The rule says, let us suppose, that when a creditor has promised not to enforce part of the debt, and the debtor has acted in reliance on that promise, the creditor may not go back on his promise. We are now confronted by a later case in which the creditor promised he would not enforce part of the debt, the debtor acted in reliance on this, and the creditor now wishes to go back on his promise. Is he debarred from doing so?

The good law student should see straight away that he cannot answer that question until he knows more of the facts. What if, in the later case, the debtor has used economic duress to extract the creditor's promise while there was no such duress in the original case? What if, in the original case, the debtor had, in reliance on the promise, *acted to his detriment*, while in the later case the debtor was not detrimentally affected (or had even profited by, for example, using the waived part of his debt to make a highly successful investment)? But if case law is just a matter of rules, *why should* it be necessary to know all the facts of the cases? Why is it not enough to know the rule that a case has established and to know that the facts specified as relevant by that rule are present in the later case? The actual process of case law reasoning can only be reconciled with the black letter rule view of law by insisting that all the later qualifications (about economic duress, detrimental reliance, etc.) were impliedly anticipated by the rule as originally declared. But the list of such qualifications is potentially infinite and could not possibly be implied by the original decision. Nor can we say that each later decision is able to modify the original rule: for a rule that is liable to be changed on every occasion that it is applied is no rule at all.

The above arguments are not intended as a knock down refutation of the black letter view of law, which is in any case too vaguely formulated a target to be worth refuting. What the arguments are intended to do is to get the student questioning his own understanding of law. Many people, after reading the arguments I have offered, will respond by saying "this is all very well, but when I silently assented to the conception of law that Simmonds has described as the black letter view, I did not have in mind anything as crude as the view he attacks". Precisely! But now I want you to start thinking about what exactly you *did* have in mind, and how exactly you would modify my crude account of the black letter view so as to meet the arguments I have offered.

Principles and justice

At this point it will be helpful to consider a conception of law that may be regarded as a rival to the black letter view. We may call this conception the "principled" view of law. On this view, the statutes and decided cases of the legal order share, to a considerable degree, a coherent moral position. The legal writer, the advocate, and the judge should, in expounding the law, assume that the statutes and cases rest on a coherent conception of justice. They should assume that underlying the established rules are certain general principles which may be unstated but which are nevertheless a part of the existing law. The law is, on this account, not just a long list of established rules, but a body of rules together with a wider conception of justice that they embody.

This way of thinking about law offers an explanation of how a case that is not clearly settled by an established rule can nevertheless be decided *according to law*: for such cases may be settled by reference to the underlying principles and conception of justice which the established rules seek to implement. It also offers an explanation of how it is that experts may disagree about the law: for the reconstruction of the moral conceptions that are embodied in the established rules is an inherently controversial task. In the law of contract, for example, one lawyer may see the rules as based on a moral position that emphasises liberty, responsibility and the sanctity of promises. He may then treat doctrines such as the doctrine of frustration as genuine attempts to implement the will of the parties. Another lawyer may treat contract as less concerned with the sanctity of promises and more concerned with questions of distributive justice between the parties. He will interpret the doctrine of frustration as being concerned to achieve a distributively just result in circumstances which were not foreseen and in relation to which the parties have no intentions. The contrast between the two views of contract will run right through the two lawyers' approaches to implied terms, mistakes, damages, and many other areas of the law. In deciding which is the *correct* view of the parties' legal rights in some difficult case, we may have to decide which is the better interpretation of the underlying moral significance of the law of contract. That is obviously a difficult and controversial task, which admits of more than one reasonable answer. In this way we can understand how experts may disagree about what the existing law of contract *is*, and not just about what it *ought to be*.

It should not be assumed at this stage that the principled view of law is committed to viewing the law as morally *right*. In saying that the law is based on this or that conception of justice, we need not endorse that conception of justice as the true or correct conception. We may hold that the law is based on a particular moral theory, while ourselves disapproving of that theory. For example, we might hold that the criminal law is based on conceptions of justice as retribution for evil, yet view such notions of justice with horror, seeing them as barbaric remnants of an inhumane thirst for revenge. Or we might see the law of contract as based on a political theory of laissez faire, while ourselves advocating a more paternalistic position.

Because the conception of justice on which the law is based need not be the correct or morally acceptable conception, there are two separate reasons why the lawyer should have some awareness of the rival theories of justice that have been offered by political theorists. On the one hand the lawyer will wish to have some understanding of the major dichotomies and problems in constructing a theory of justice because this will help him in presenting the legal materials as themselves based on some coherent notion of justice. For example, suppose that someone argued that it is wrong to treat the law of contract as based on a morality emphasising freedom and the binding nature of promises since that interpretation would render the law of contract inconsistent with the values underlying paternalistic consumer legislation as well as the paternalistic and redistributive welfare state. To evaluate this suggestion, we would need to ask whether it is right to regard consumer and welfare laws as paternalistic, and whether egalitarian redistribution is inconsistent with the values of freedom of contract. The answers to these questions are by no means obvious, and they demand an understanding of political theory.

It is even more obvious that, *whatever* view of law we hold, we must engage in philosophical reflection about morality and justice if we are responsibly to evaluate and criticise the existing laws. This is so whether we take the black letter view, the principled view, or any other. Accordingly, in Part I of this book, an attempt will be made to indicate to the student the most significant alternative theories that have been offered as accounts of justice and moral right. In Part II closer attention will be given to the concept of law itself.

Coherence, rules and illusions

As we have seen, the principled view of law does not assume that the existing law is morally right. But it does appear to assume that the law is to a large extent *consistent* and that it rests on some coherent conception of justice, albeit a conception that we may disagree with. This assumption is not self-evidently justified, and may be rejected as unacceptable. On the one hand it may be argued that the law does not in fact exhibit a high degree of coherence: that different rules serve different policies which collectively amount to a muddle rather than a conception of justice. On the other hand it may be argued that even if legal systems generally do exhibit a high degree of coherence in the underlying purposes of their rules, this is not a *necessary* feature of law and so should not be built in to the *concept* of law. On whichever basis the argument is put it amounts for our purposes to the same thing: "the law" should be taken to be the established black letter rules, and not any wider concepts or principles which could be extrapolated from those rules as forming the conception of justice on which the rules are based.

This objection to the principled view, with the latter's assumption of coherence in the law, can be given a directly political significance in the following way. We saw earlier that the principled view was able to explain how cases not covered by established black letter rules might nevertheless be decided according to law, since they could be decided by reference to the conception of justice on which the rules are based. But if the rules are in fact *not* based on any such conception (or if that conception is not properly part of *the law*), this account of how such cases are decided will not suffice. Yet if this account is rejected, are we to conclude that cases not covered by established rules are not decided according to law? Does it follow that they are decided according to the judge's personal values and beliefs? Why should unelected officials such as judges enjoy this kind of power?

This problem of judicial discretion in cases not covered by clear rules might be thought to be a tricky but not an unfamiliar one. We are quite used to the idea that judges do *not* just apply rules but also make and shape them; we believe, therefore, that judges exercise

7

discretionary power, and in many cases we are prepared to justify such power by a variety of pragmatic arguments. But the problem runs deeper than this.

If we reject the principled view of law, we might claim that only the black letter rules actually count as "law". We will then feel that the discretionary power exercised by judges is a problem that arises only in the minority of cases that are not clearly covered by a rule. Arising only in a minority of cases it is perhaps justifiable consistently with democratic principles, provided that the latter are spiced with a touch of pragmatism.

This seemingly commonsensical position is, however, not an easy one to maintain. For, once we have rejected all arguments about coherence and underlying principles, consigning them to the lumber room of "not law", we will find it hard to avoid sending all the black letter rules the same way. Consider the example described above of the creditor's promise not to claim a part of his debt. A court might treat the earlier precedent as establishing a rule to the following effect: "if a creditor promises not to enforce a part of the debt and the debtor acts in reliance on this, the creditor is bound by his promise". Yet the court would feel quite happy to create a new exception to the rule so as to exempt from its scope a creditor whose promise was extracted by undue financial pressure from the debtor. Or take an example from Lon Fuller. A rule prohibits vehicles from the municipal park. The present case involves a lorry in the municipal park. Well, a lorry is clearly a vehicle and might be thought to be clearly caught by the rule. But, Fuller points out, if the vehicle were being installed as a memorial by war veterans a court might hold that it was not affected by the rule, as falling outside its intended scope.

By developing examples such as these one can argue that *whenever* a court is faced with a clear rule, and a case apparently falling within the rule, the court can avoid applying the rule if it wishes. If a court can always avoid applying the rule (it is argued) it must be the case that it applies the rule only when it *wants* to. Now a rule that I apply only when I want to is not a rule that I am bound by: it is, in fact, not a genuine rule at all. The extreme conclusion that the argument leads us to is the view that courts are never bound by rules and that rules are, in reality, of no importance in determining the court's decision. A court, on this view, can do whatever it chooses. The invocation of rules, and the elaborate discussion of rules in judgments and academic textbooks, both reflects and perpetuates an illusion concealing the naked exercise of uncontrolled power by the judiciary. This position has been labelled "rule-scepticism".

Suppose that someone tried to refute rule-scepticism this way. "In both the examples you give," he might argue "we have the court interpreting the rule in the light of its purpose. The rule about the creditor's waiver was established in order to avoid inequitable results where the creditor goes back on his promise: it was not intended to apply where it would *not* be inequitable to allow the creditor to go back on his promise. In the case of the lorry it is even more clear that the rule was not intended to apply to such a case but to exclude noise and traffic hazards from the park, neither of which will be produced by a memorial. Neither of these examples demonstrates that courts are not bound by rules: merely that they must apply the rules in the light of their purposes."

This is a good reply. But does it not lead to the conclusion that the law consists not only of rules but of rules plus their purposes? If the purpose is something the court must have regard to and which plays an integral part in the court's legal reasoning, what warrant have we for not treating the purpose as itself a part of the law? And if underlying purposes are to be treated as part of the law along with the black letter rules, are we not coming close to the principled view that we started by rejecting? In order to get all the way back to the principled view we need only suggest that legal purposes are not discreet, so that each rule has a distinct and separable purpose, but that the purposes of each rule must be understood in the light of the wider purposes served by the area of law to which it belongs. And this is surely true: for we cannot hope to form a view on the purpose of the doctrine of frustration, for example, if we know nothing of how that doctrine fits into the other rules of the law of contract and into the general purposes of contract law.

Thus we have seen that the rejection of the principled view of law can lead to a rejection of the black letter view as well, and the adoption of an extreme and somewhat puzzling rule-scepticism. The black letter view seems closest to most of our untutored images of law, but it is much more difficult to maintain consistently than we at first imagined. We have however been treating these rival conceptions of law in an unforgiveably thin and unhistorical manner. Before we conclude this introduction it will be as well to offer a brief sketch of some of the historical background to the modern jurisprudential debate and to explain more fully the range of issues over which that debate moves.

Rights, rules and utility

We usually think of law as requiring systematic study. We assume that law is not merely a long list of separate rules, or a jumble of unrelated decided cases, but an ordered body of standards exhibiting some degree of structure and system. Why should we make these assumptions? How exactly does law differ from a long list of rules?

Historically the assumed systematic character of law has been strongly influenced by the tradition of natural law theory. It has been said that modern legal textbook writers are the heirs to the natural law tradition in so far as they seek to expound the detailed rules of law in relation to underlying principles and values. Certainly we can find legal writers of the seventeenth and eighteenth centuries invoking theories of natural law as a justification for their attempt to expound the law in ordered principles. Generally speaking, natural law theories in this period held that men had certain natural rights and duties, the enforcement of which made organised social life possible. Courts and legal systems have the task of defining and then enforcing these natural rights and duties. To the extent that it was based on principles of reason and justice, the law was capable of systematic study and exposition, since the various established rules could be related to underlying principles that they expressed, or rights that they protected.

Many of the modern debates in jurisprudence find their most immediate origin in the attack that was mounted on natural law theories, at the end of the eighteenth century, by Jeremy Bentham. Bentham argued that talk of natural law and of natural rights could settle nothing: there was no way of demonstrating what such laws and rights might be, and so the theory of natural law offered no determinate guidance on moral and political issues. The only proper basis for determining how we should live, what laws we should have, and so forth, was the principle of utility. This principle held that one should always act so as to maximise the greatest happiness of the greatest number. The only good reason for a law was its tendency to maximise happiness: all talk of law as enforcing pre-existing natural rights was not only wasted breath but also positively harmful, as diverting men's attention from the real issue of the consequences for welfare of having this or that law.

Bentham's rejection of natural law and his adoption of the principle of utility led him to further controversial conclusions. As we have already noted, the great legal writers of the period tended to expound the law in terms of an underlying natural law theory. Thus Blackstone's *Commentaries on the Laws of England* presented the major features of English law as an embodiment and protection of certain basic natural rights. Bentham objected to this approach because, he held, it confused the *existence* of a law with its merit or demerit. Whether or not a certain rule was an existing rule of English law depended upon whether that rule had been laid down. But whether or not it was a *good* law was an altogether separate issue, depending on the tendency of the law to maximise happiness. An approach that treated positive law expressly laid down in established rules as a manifestation of natural law was objectionable in that it confused what the law *is* with what the law morally *ought* to be. Since the conception of law as embodying underlying principles was, at this period, itself an aspect of the idea that positive law embodied natural law, Bentham rejected that conception. The theory of law that he constructed admitted only positive black letter rules as a part of the existing law. All doctrinal arguments that were not concerned with the application of black letter rules were treated by Bentham as arguments about what the law should be, but not about what it is.

Bentham's critique of natural law theory thus gave rise to a number of problems that have continued to occupy the centre of the stage in modern jurisprudential debates. First and foremost is the question of the separation of the law as it is and as it ought to be. When we state that someone has such and such a legal duty, are we making a kind of moral judgment? In describing the law as imposing a duty, are we committed to saying that the law is morally right? Those who wish to answer "no" to both of these questions are generally called "legal positivists". Legal positivists do not wish to argue that morality does not influence the law, or that law is not subject to moral scrutiny and criticism, nor would they necessarily deny that we may have a moral obligation to obey the law. What they do wish to claim is that the mere fact that something is the law does not make it right. The concept of law, for positivists, is a concept with no intrinsic moral connotations.

Second is the question of how we are to conceive of the nature of legal standards. Does law consist entirely of rules that have been expressly established in black letter form? Or can the law be said to include principles that have never been expressly formulated, but which are believed to form part of the conception of justice on which the black letter rules are based? We have already seen some of the problems that arise in relation to this issue.

Third is the principle of utility itself. We will see in Part I of this

11

book that the principle of utility as an account of morality faces serious difficulty. It can be argued that adherence to the principle would lead to morally abhorrent action in certain circumstances. It can also be argued that general adherence to the principle would make social co-ordination impossible, since such co-ordination requires a framework of rules that are treated as binding, irrespective of the requirements of utility. It can be suggested that utility is strangely irrelevant to the problem of justice, since the principle of utility is indifferent to questions of distribution which are central to the concept of justice, and because justice is concerned with largely backward looking considerations, not with the future consequences taken account of by utility. Later in Part I, we will consider some rival attempts to develop theories of justice. The theoretical problems of justice are important for the lawyer not only in themselves but also, as we shall see, for the bearing that they have on the concept of law itself.

All of these issues are important, not as a diversion from the more mundane parts of legal study, nor as an attempt to broaden the lawyer's education. They are problems that run through the fabric of legal argument itself and have a bearing on legal study at every point. Without an understanding of these basic issues, no proper understanding of law is possible.

Part One

Justice

Justice

1. Utilitarianism

There are a great many different moral and political theories which fall under the general heading of utilitarianism, and it will obviously not be possible to discuss all of them, or even a representative selection of them. For the purposes of this book it is enough to isolate certain features which are common to all such theories, and to indicate in brief terms some of the major divergencies and alternative lines of development that have been pursued in different individual theories. The classical utilitarian theories (of Bentham, J. S. Mill and, perhaps, Henry Sidgwick) took the fundamental basis of morality to be a requirement that happiness should be maximised: the basic principle of utility required us to weigh up the consequences, in terms of happiness and unhappiness, of various alternative actions, and choose that action which would, on balance, have the best consequences, in the sense of producing the largest net balance of happiness. Later theories have sometimes abandoned the notion of happiness in favour of other values, or have modified the account of how exactly the principle of utility is to be brought to bear on individual actions. I shall describe some of these modifications in general terms later in this chapter. But since all utilitarian theories are concerned with making people "better off" in some sense, I shall use the term "welfare" as a general label which does not distinguish between happiness and other values that replace that notion in more modern theories.

Utilitarianism has been a profoundly influential theory, and it could not have achieved this influence if it did not reflect, in some way and to some extent, important features of our moral beliefs. It is worth starting by tracing some of the fundamental intuitions and ideas that lend initial plausibility to utilitarianism. For example, we assume that the business of reflecting on what we morally ought to do, and of subjecting to moral scrutiny the actions of others, is not a pointless activity, but has some general purpose or significance. What purpose could that be if not the purpose of making the world a better place? And what could be more important from *that* point of view than the maximisation of human welfare, or perhaps the welfare of all sentient beings? But if the whole point of morality is to maximise welfare, then surely the basic principle of morality must be a requirement of welfare maximisation. Again, if we reflect on accepted moral standards such as the requirements that we should not kill, or cause unnecessary pain, or break our promises, we may ask "why are all these actions regarded as wrong?" One answer is "because they all cause harm and suffering, and make people worse off": and *that* suggests, once again, that the basis of morality is a concern with welfare, with making people better off.

Certain general features of utilitarianism will be explored in this chapter, and may be outlined at this point. For example, utilitarianism is exclusively future-looking, in the sense that it evaluates actions solely by reference to their likely consequences and not at all by reference to past events, except insofar as those events have a bearing on the future. We ordinarily assume that I may be morally bound to do something because of a promise that I made: but a utilitarian will argue that *in itself* the promise cannot constitute a reason for action of any kind. If I am morally bound to keep the promise this is not because of the bare fact of having made it, but because of the harmful consequences that my act of promise-breaking is likely to cause. Many of these harmful consequences will only occur because I made the promise in the first place, *e.g.* some people may have been induced to rely on me, and may be harmed as a result of my failure to keep my word: but the past event of the promise is relevant only by virtue of such consequences, and not in itself.

Allied to the exclusive concern with future consequences is the utilitarian's positive attitude towards welfare. Whether he understands welfare as a matter of happiness, as a matter of the attainment of preferences, or in some other way, the utilitarian always regards welfare as a "good thing", to be increased if possible. The only acceptable reason for making someone worse off than he might otherwise be, according to the utilitarian, is if we can in this way improve the welfare of others to an extent that outweighs the first person's loss.

Being concerned only to *maximise* welfare, the utilitarian is not (as we shall see) concerned with how the welfare is distributed. If the sum total of human welfare can be increased only by producing inequalities in welfare, the utilitarian will go for maximisation, rather than equal distribution. This is sometimes regarded as a weakness in utilitarianism, since it is argued that questions of distribution are the crucial questions of justice, and that lack of concern with such issues shows a degree of moral blindness in the utilitarian. But we will discover that the utilitarian has a challenging and provocative reply at his disposal, to the effect that only considerations of utility can explain why distributive issues matter at all.

This last argument points to another striking feature of utilitarianism. It is *monistic*, in the sense that it holds that morality is based on one supreme principle. By contrast, pluralistic theories hold that there are a number of distinct principles, or values that must be traded off against each other. For example we would usually think of liberty, equality, and economic efficiency as values that are important but different, and that may come into conflict with each other. When they do conflict, we may feel it is necessary to "strike a balance" between them, without any determinate principles to guide us. The utilitarian will treat all of these values as important only insofar as they bear on the maximisation of welfare, and will handle apparent conflict between them simply by applying his supreme principle.

Consequences

Utilitarianism holds that, in deciding what we should do, we should consider only the consequences of our actions: an action cannot be justified purely by its relationship to past facts. An example will make this clearer.

Suppose that I am stranded on a desert island with one other man, who is dying. In his last hours he entrusts me with a large sum of money and asks me to give it to his daughter if I ever manage to return to England. I agree to this arrangement. Eventually I am rescued and arrive back in England. I find the man's daughter and I discover that she is already fabulously rich. The money I have for her, which seemed a large amount to me, will be scarcely noticed by her. I begin to wonder whether I would not do more good by giving most of the money to charity, rather than by giving it all to the castaway's daughter.

Now, according to utilitarianism, I am at least asking the right question. I must consider whether breaking my promise would do more good than keeping it. But the utilitarian will insist that I should not assume that this question is easy to answer. The system of making and keeping promises has itself great value for human welfare, and acts of promise-breaking will tend to undermine that system and so have adverse effects on welfare. If people come to hear of frequent acts of promise-breaking, like the one I contemplate, they will be less inclined to rely on promises in the future; and, even if I keep the facts completely secret, my decision to break the promise may weaken my own propensity to keep promises in the future. These are the possible consequences of my actions that I must weigh against the benefits of giving the money to charity.

It can be argued that utilitarianism misses the central feature of the whole situation: that is, that I have *promised* to give the money to the castaway's daughter. The reason why I *ought* to give the money to her is not some future consequence of my action but a past fact: the fact of my having promised. After all, we may say, it is odd that I should feel free to decide for myself what will be the best way of doing good with the money: for the money was not given to me to do good generally but for me to give it to a specific person. The very evaluation of consequences required by the utilitarian approach is, on this view, one that I have no right to engage in.

The utilitarian will insist that he does take account of the past fact of the promise, but only insofar as it affects the total consequences of the contemplated act of giving away the money. His opponent will argue that all the claims about general weakening of the system of promise-breaking are not only artificial and tortuous, but also immoral in that they suggest that secret promise-breaking may be justifiable when open and declared promise-breaking would not.

Opponents of utilitarianism face a difficulty at this point however. Very few people would hold that the duty to keep promises is absolute: most of us would feel that it may be overridden in certain circumstances. Suppose, for example, that I have promised to take you to the theatre for an evening, but quite unexpectedly my help is needed at an emergency. We would generally feel that the duty to help in the emergency overrides the duty to keep my promise and that I act properly in breaking that promise. Yet how can that be if the morality of keeping promises is not ultimately based on a calculation of consequences? The utilitarian can explain such situations quite easily (perhaps too easily) but an approach which treats the act of promising as taking away the *right* to evaluate the pros and cons of keeping the promise will have much more difficulty.

Suppose we argue along the following line. When I made the promise to take you to the theatre, you could not have thought that I was promising to do so come what may. If, for example, I had myself been seriously injured you would not expect me to struggle out of hospital in a wheelchair in order to take you. This is because (we might argue) the promise was made subject to certain implied and unspecified exceptions. When I helped with the emergency instead of taking you to the theatre, I was not really breaking my promise but relying on an implied exception to it.

The notion of an implied exception to a promise, of unspecified extent, and covering eventualities that I did not contemplate for one moment at the time of making the promise, may be thought to be a nonsense. It would be wrong however to jump to this conclusion. To say that I meant this or that by my promise need not imply conscious advertance on my part. As Wittgenstein points out, if I ask someone to "show the children a game", and the person requested teaches them gambling with dice, I may truthfully say that I did not mean *that* sort of game, even though the possibility of their being taught such a game had never occured to me. Similarly I may say that when I promised to take you to the theatre I did not promise to do so come hell or high water and I never intended that the promise should apply to emergency situations. The truth of my statement would not be affected by the fact that I never even contemplated the possibility of an emergency arising.

The "implied exception" approach may, however, go too far, for it suggests that, properly understood, my act of helping at the emergency was not a breach of the promise I made to you at all. That promise, it is argued, did not apply in these circumstances, and so I did not break it. But we may feel that this is a misguided approach. I *have* broken my promise to you and perhaps I should do something to compensate. Neil MacCormick has argued that there is an obligation to compensate for the effects of certain actions which are not themselves wrongful acts, and a breach of promise in these circumstances would be a good example. The utilitarian on the other hand with his exclusive focus on consequences will argue that whether or not one should be required to pay compensation for a breach of contract (or to buy a bunch of flowers as compensation for a missed trip to the theatre) should be evaluated by the overall consequences of requiring such compensation, just as the rightness or wrongness of breaking the promise itself is to be evaluated by reference to its consequences. I have used the example of promising not only because it casts light on the exclusive concern of the utilitarian with the future consequences of actions, but also because it should help the student to see the possible bearing that these arguments may have on an area of law like the law of contract.

Arguments about the nature of implied terms, the basis of the doctrine of frustration, the basis of damages in contract and the general rationale of the distinction between private law damages and criminal law penalties are inextricably intertwined with the philosophical problems we are discussing. Some suggestions for further reading on these questions are made at the end of the chapter.

Positive view of welfare

One of the most immediately attractive aspects of utilitarianism is the highly positive view that it takes of welfare. Utilitarians may conceive of welfare in different ways but on any account welfare is always a good thing. Classical utilitarians such as Jeremy Bentham held that utility required the maximisation of happiness, which he tended to identify with pleasurable experiences (or, rather, the balance of pleasurable experiences over painful ones). Bentham held that pleasure is always a good thing and that the fact that an act produces pleasure is always a reason (though not necessarily a *conclusive* reason) for doing it. In order to decide whether an act should be done, Bentham held we should assess all the likely consequences of the act for everyone, weighing the pleasurable experiences against the painful ones. Having assessed the likely effect of our act on the pleasure and pain of everyone concerned we should perform the act only if it maximises the total balance of pleasure over pain.

This apparently attractive feature of utilitarianism may however seem slightly less appealing on reflection. It can be argued for example that the activities of a sadist will be regarded as wrong by the utilitarian only because the sadist does not derive sufficient pleasure from his actions. It is because the harmful consequences of sadism outweigh the happiness (if we may so style it) accruing to the sadist that the utilitarian regards sadism as wrong. Opponents of utilitarianism feel that this is the wrong reason for condemning the sadist's actions. A number of points can be made, as follows.

1. We are invited by the utilitarian to weigh the pleasure of the sadist against his victim's pain. But how is this to be done? Even if such inter-personal comparisons of pleasure and pain are possible, they seem bound to be highly speculative and uncertain. Yet we are absolutely certain that the sadist is acting wrongly, and that certainty cannot plausibly be based

on an uncertain and speculative investigation into the degree of pleasure he derives.

2. In Bentham's elaborate classification of types of pleasure he gives "the pleasures of malevolence". Bentham holds that even pleasures such as these, like the pleasures of the sadist, should count positively in favour of an act. This is hard to accept intuitively. The fact that people drøol over and delight in scenes of cruelty and horror is a reason against their activities, not in favour of them. But the classical utilitarian must count all pleasures as on a par, all counting equally in favour of the acts that produce them.

   More recently, utilitarians have sought ways of avoiding these difficulties. The notion of "happiness" or "pleasure" has been replaced by the idea of satisfying one's preferences, and the general principle has been taken to be "maximise the extent to which people may satisfy their own preferences". It can be argued that some preferences are irrational and should not be given any weight in the utilitarian calculus. If we can treat the sadist's preferences as irrational, we need not place any value on them. There are many difficulties with an approach of this kind. We will see later that "preference" utilitarianism creates difficulties of its own, and the added willingness to denounce some preferences as irrational threatens to seriously dilute utilitarianism, as well as having highly autocratic political implications.

3. Suppose that the sadist actually derived enormous pleasure from inflicting merely slight discomfort on his victims: say, by boring them with his holiday snaps or with lengthy descriptions of his new Volvo. Does that make his activity justifiable, even though it is done without the victim's consent (the victim is, let us say, strapped into a chair, or locked in a garage with only the Volvo to look at and hear about)? Surely, we may feel, people are not entitled to simply *use* us, without our consent, simply because they can in some way derive pleasure from us. From this point of view the pleasure and pain flowing from the sadist's activities is an irrelevance. His act, being done without our consent, is a violation of our rights and *that* is what makes it wrong.

As we shall see in Chapter 2, John Rawls argues that utilitarianism makes the mistake of defining the right in terms of the good. He means that the utilitarian starts with an account of what is good (pleasure, happiness, obtaining one's preferences, etc.) and then says that an action is right insofar as it maximises that good. Against this approach, Rawls argues that rules of justice are prior to the good. We can arrive at certain principles of justice which are independent of any particular conception of what is a good or worthwhile life. Such principles provide a framework within which people's conception of the good must be pursued. We can therefore only decide whether positive moral value attaches to a certain form of pleasure when we know how it is related to the basic principles of justice. For this reason, Rawls would regard as valid the objection that the sadist's pleasure must be discounted because it is obtained in violation of basic principles of justice.

Rationality

A powerful strand of thinking which has tended to support utilitarian theories is the idea that rationality is almost entirely a matter of fitting means to ends in an instrumental manner. This conception of reason is historically associated with the name of David Hume, the eighteenth century Scottish philosopher. In fact Hume's position is both more radical and more complex than is usually assumed, but there is some truth in the conventional understanding of his theory, and it is that conventional picture that I shall describe as "the Humean conception of reason".

Hume argued that reason cannot tell us what we ought to pursue, but only how to attain ends we have already chosen. Thus reason can tell me that, if I want to keep dry on a rainy day, I ought to carry an umbrella. Reason can also tell me that, if I want to stay fit and healthy, I should avoid getting wet (and so should carry an umbrella, etc.). But reason cannot tell me whether fitness and health are things worth pursuing. I simply have to decide for myself what I want: do I want to be healthy, happy, etc.? If I should decide that I do not want to be healthy, happy, or even alive, no one can accuse me of being irrational, provided that I am fully informed of the relevant facts and have not based my preferences on false factual beliefs.

Some eighteenth century writers had argued that reason could demonstrate certain basic moral propositions, such as "promises ought to be kept", to be true. Hume rejected such theories since they relied upon a wildly exaggerated idea of what human reason could achieve. Ultimately, Hume argued, our moral beliefs must be based on preferences, such as the preference for an orderly society where promises are kept and therefore commercial life and material prosperity is possible. Such preferences are themselves neither reasonable nor unreasonable: they are merely given facts of human nature. But what if human nature has a certain uniformity, so that there are some things that all men desire? The classical utilitarians argued that there was indeed one thing that all men desired, and that was happiness. In fact, they argued, everything that a man desires, he desires because he believes that it will bring him happiness. Happiness is the underlying purpose of all human actions on this view. If human action is to be rational, it should aim to maximise happiness. All talk of justice and rights as something independent of the concern to maximise happiness is a ridiculous and dangerous diversion from the real demands of morality.

Now there are a very large number of ways in which this argument can be attacked, but let us notice only two of them, which are immediately relevant to the themes of this book.

Some theorists, such as the Oxford lawyer and philosopher John Finnis, would argue that reason does indicate certain goals that ought to be pursued, and that happiness is at best only one of these goals. Nor does Finnis's theory simply turn out to be a more complex version of utilitarianism, with a list of "goods" substituting for the single good of happiness. Finnis argues that the various objective goods prescribed by reason are *incommensurable*: that is, we cannot weigh or measure one good against another. In view of this, he argues, the injunction to maximise the good makes no sense. The bearing that his account of objective goods has on individual conduct is more complex than straightforward maximisation. Finnis's theory will be described later in Part I of this book.

Another fundamental objection to the argument from the Humean conception of reason to utilitarianism claims that the argument ignores the distinction between prudential and moral reasons. A prudential reason is a reason for action framed in terms of the actor's own interests. Thus I may have a prudential reason for carrying an umbrella in order to keep dry, because keeping dry is in my interest. But *moral* reasons are frequently, and indeed usually, independent of the actor's own interest. I have a moral reason to visit my friend because I promised to do so. Whether or not it is in my interest to visit her is not immediately relevant to this reason. If my reason for visiting her is because I think she will give me some money, my reason for visiting her is not a moral but a prudential one. The idea that all men desire happiness, and that reason requires us to adopt the most effective means to that end, certainly explains

23

why the actor might have a reason to maximise his *own* happiness. But why should he maximise the happiness of other people? Does reason require that? Utilitarianism does not prescribe universal egotism, but a concern for the welfare of all persons (or all sentient beings).

The major theorists of utilitarianism attempted to grapple with this problem in various ways. Sidgwick thought of the principle of utility as itself based on a fundamental moral intuition, and thought that reason alone could not determine the choice between egoism and utilitarianism. Jeremy Bentham thought of the individual actor as egoistic, but he argued that morality was a system of rules that it was in everyone's interest to support, at least to the extent of censuring the immorality of others (such censure thus providing a system of sanctions inducing compliance). But it is not my present purpose to explore these responses, nor the still more subtle (some would say muddled) attempts of John Stuart Mill to confront the problem. Rather, I wish to suggest that serious attention to the contrast between moral and prudential reasons can lead us to a quite different conception of rationality from the Humean one.

We are in effect asking "why should I be moral? Why not just act out of prudence, ignoring the interests of others except insofar as it pleases me to notice them?" This is the most fundamental question for moral philosophy and will lead us into waters that are of formidable depth, especially for the law student. But with a little courage and patience some light may be cast on an intractable problem.

Let us begin by asking a question about prudence. I say that it is prudent to carry an umbrella and that I therefore have a reason to do so. At this moment, however, the sun is shining, an umbrella is a nuisance, and I do not *want* to carry one. I have heard a weather forecast and I am expecting rain. I know that, without my umbrella, I will get wet. But why should I *now* care about what will happen to me later in the day? The short answer is that I am the same person now that will later be getting wet if I take no umbrella. In other words, the rationality of prudence rests on a particular conception of the person. In treating prudence as rational we are accepting that persons do not simply exist for an instant to be replaced by other persons: they have a continuous identity through time. We may call this the notion of the continuing persona.

Now let us ask about the rationality of moral concern for others. Why should I concern myself with the interests of other people? How can their interests give me a reason for action? In the case of prudence we saw that the rationality of prudence rested on a particular conception of the person as continuous through time. Similarly, the rationality of morality rests on a conception of the person as inhabiting a world of other persons. This is not simply a *fact* about the person: it does not just happen to be the case that one inhabits a world of other persons. There are good philosophical grounds for holding that nothing that could be regarded as a *person* could exist except in a world of other persons. Thus one may argue that being in a world of other persons is logically entailed by the concept of a person.

This argument leads us to the conclusion that the rationality of morality is just as deep and well grounded as the rationality of prudence. Each form of reason rests on an aspect of the person. Prudence presupposes the person's continuity, while morality presupposes the person's *universality i.e.* the fact that one can be a person only in a world of other persons. I shall call this the notion of the moral persona.

The notion of the moral persona provides us with an explanation of morality, and could certainly be used to underpin a utilitarian theory. Yet it might equally suggest a quite different type of theory, radically opposed to utilitarianism. This type of theory may be labelled "Kantian", because it is historically associated with the philosophy of Immanuel Kant (though I do not claim to be offering an exposition of Kant's actual views).

A Kantian moral theory holds that the basic moral requirement is to act with respect for persons. If we think of a person as being capable of choices, plans and projects of his own, we may interpret the idea of respect for persons in the following way. One should never treat another person purely as a means to your own goals and objectives, but should always respect the fact that that person has his own goals and objectives. Inevitably, a theory of this kind places a high emphasis on liberty, and stresses the importance of not interfering with the liberty of a person merely because it would make him or someone else better off. Liberty should be interfered with only to restrain violations of liberty. Thus I can interfere with your liberty to assault me because, in doing so, I interfere only with an attempted violation of liberty: I interfere with you only insofar as that is necessary to maintain equal liberty for everyone. Utilitarianism, on the other hand, would licence any interference with liberty that was likely to improve overall welfare. Further, utilitarianism in its classical form itself seems to rest on a fundamental judgment about what is good and worth pursuing (happiness) and may therefore be regarded as displaying lack of respect for the projects and aspirations of individual persons.

Liberalism, happiness and preferences

On the basis of the preceding account of moral rationality we may say that the foundation of morality is a requirement of respect for persons. To some extent, utilitarianism and Kantian moral theory may be regarded as rival interpretations of this requirement. Viewing the theories in this way helps us to assess their rival merits, and helps us to see certain fundamental problems in the utilitarian standpoint.

Utilitarianism may claim to embody the notion of respect for persons in the following way. When he calculates the likely consequences of his actions in terms of welfare or happiness, the utilitarian takes account of everyone's interests. It may be that, in extreme cases, the utilitarian might approve of actions that seriously harm particular individuals: but this will not be because the interests of those individuals have been ignored. Rather, their interests will have been considered and given equal weight along with the interests of everyone else. If the infliction of harm is justified it is justified because its beneficial consequences for the general welfare outweigh its harmful ones. The utilitarian can argue that this is the only plausible way of expressing respect for persons in one's conduct. To refuse to harm the individual even when that will serve the general welfare is to *fail* to attach equal importance to the interests of everyone: it is to allow *this individual's* interests to weigh more heavily than do the interests of others.

This can seem a convincing argument. If we find it plausible we may conclude that the notion of respect for persons is quite consistent with utilitarianism. But before we reach that conclusion we should pause to consider some deeper problems.

It is true that utilitarianism allows each person's interests to count equally. But does utilitarianism exhibit respect for persons in constructing its account of what constitutes each person's interests? The utilitarian begins, it would seem, with an account of welfare, and then seeks to maximise welfare as so defined. He may, for example, regard happiness or pleasure as the most important thing, and then seek to increase the sum total of happiness in the world. Or he may offer some other account of the "good" that is to be maximised. A theory that is constructed in this way does not attach

26

sufficient importance to the capacity of each person to decide for himself on a conception of "the good", to choose his own aspirations and ideals. Utilitarianism appears to choose *one* goal or ideal in terms of which it assesses everyone's interests. Thus, for the classical utilitarian, an artist's wish to paint is of moral importance only insofar as it will yield happiness for the artist or his customers. But the artist might not accept this characterisation of his aim. Happiness, for him, might *not* be the point.

Is there a way in which the utilitarian can avoid imposing one conception of the good on everyone, including those who do not accept it? There is one possibility, represented by what I shall describe as "preference-utilitarianism". This theory holds that one should seek to maximise, not happiness, but the extent to which people can attain their own preferences, whatever those preferences may be.

Preference-utilitarianism has the virtue of being close to the liberal spirit of the classical utilitarians such as Bentham and Mill. Some political theories hold that the basic question one must ask, before offering a theory of justice and politics, concerns the issue of what is truly valuable and good. On this view we should begin by asking what goals and aspirations are genuinely worthwhile, what ways of living would count as excellence in a human being. Having in this way arrived at a "conception of the good", we should then seek to devise laws and institutions that will encourage the attainment of that good. If, for example, we believe that communal activity is good and truly valuable, and that individual activity is less good, we will advocate a society that fosters communal activity and discourages individualism. Liberal political theories reject this general approach. They hold that our account of the principles of justice and moral right (and our choice of laws and institutions) should not presuppose any particular conception of what is a good and worthwhile life. The mere fact that we believe that one way of life is valuable and ought to be aspired to, while another way of life is not, does not justify us in imposing that view on others by making it the presupposed basic value of our legal and political system. Rather than seeking to inculcate and encourage *one* conception of the good life, the law should, so far as possible, provide a framework within which everyone has the opportunity to pursue his own conception of the good life.

A brief way of expressing this liberal point of view is to say that the legal order of a liberal society should be *neutral* between different conceptions of the good. But saying this can encourage a popular

27

and fallacious objection to liberalism, which it will be as well to note at this point. The opponents of liberalism frequently object that the claim of liberal laws to neutrality is false and hypocritical. Inevitably they must prohibit the pursuit of *some* conceptions of the good. The law must, for example, prohibit the psychopathic killer from pursuing *his* idea of a good life (*i.e.* one spent killing). And in fact, it is argued, liberal political systems inevitably discriminate unfairly *in favour* of those conceptions of the good that emphasise individual self-seeking and materialistic gain, and *against* those conceptions that emphasise the value of communal life and of living in a community of caring and compassionate altruists. This objection to liberalism is fallacious because it misconceives the nature of the neutrality that is claimed by the liberal legal order. The legal order of a liberal society can never allow everyone to pursue his own conception of the good. But the restraints that the legal order imposes need not presuppose that one conception is *true* and another *false*. Thus, the activities of the killer will be prohibited *not* because we believe the killer to have an inadequate or unacceptable notion of a good life, but because his activities necessarily interfere with the ability of others to pursue their own conception of the good. This also serves to explain why liberal theories can appear to be biased in favour of individualistic self-interest and against more communal aspirations. The person whose conception of the good involves living in a certain type of community, where others behave in certain ways towards him, has preferences that relate not just to his own life but to how other people lead *their* lives. If he can achieve his aspirations by means of the consent of other persons, well and good. If other persons do not consent, he cannot achieve his aspirations. The man with more materialistic goals is clearly in a better position here, for he is not dependent in the same way on the consent of others.

In terms of the contrast between liberal and non-liberal theories as I have described it, one might conclude that utilitarianism in its classical form was a non-liberal theory. After all, the classical utilitarian decided that happiness was *good*, and then chose laws and institutions that would maximise happiness. But the classical utilitarians are generally regarded as liberals. The liberalism of their theories was preserved by their allegiance to a maxim in terms of which the principle of utility was to be interpreted. The maxim held that each person is the best judge of his own happiness. In other words, it was assumed that if X wants a fast, shiny sports car or wants to swim the Channel, this is because these things will make her happy, and she is the best judge of that. Adherence to this maxim ensured that the classical utilitarians attached overriding importance to people's preferences, and would not seek to ignore those preferences by invoking a superior conception of the good.

The problem with this approach is that the maxim that each person is the best judge of his own happiness is quite possibly false. What if we were convinced that the maxim *was* false, and that *we* were the best judges of what would be best for some other person: would we feel justified in ignoring that person's expressed wishes and "doing him good" even without his consent? This seems too insecure and inappropriate a basis on which to rest our concern with human liberty and the autonomous choices of others. It is for reasons of this kind, amongst others, that many utilitarians have abandoned the classical emphasis on happiness in favour of a more explicitly liberal version of utilitarianism that attaches central importance to preferences.

Preference-utilitarianism raises a number of problems. For example, if we seek to maximise the attainment of preferences, are we to attach positive importance to objectionable preferences such as the preference of a racist for a society where black people are confined to subordinate and badly paid positions? The utilitarian need not be committed to *satisfying* such preferences, since they may be outweighed by other preferences of other people: but he does seem to be committed to *taking account* of such preferences when he is calculating the probable utility of a proposed action. It may be argued against the utilitarian that racist preferences should not be taken account of in this way. The fact that people hold racist preferences does not provide even the weakest of arguments in favour of a system that satisfies those preferences.

Some preference-utilitarians may try to distinguish between personal and external preferences. Personal preferences are preferences about what you acquire or what you are able to do. External preferences are preferences about what other people require or are allowed to do. Thus, a white racist may have personal preferences for a big car and lots of money; he may also have an external preference that blacks should *not* drive big cars and have lots of money. It can be argued that the utilitarian should take account only of personal preferences, and should not attach importance to external preferences. Assuming that the personal/external distinction can be clearly drawn (which we may doubt) this would deal with the problem of the racist. We should note that this approach would also exclude other preferences that we may consider less objectionable. Suppose that Sophie wishes to live in a community of caring and compassionate persons who enjoy sharing and communal life generally. Sophie's preferences incorporate preferences about other people's behaviour (other people should be caring, should share things, should live communally, etc.) and would therefore be excluded from consideration as external preferences.

Ronald Dworkin has argued that the exclusion of external preferences provides a good justification for the existence of legal restraints on the legislative power of the democratic majority, in the form of a basic Bill of Rights. We should confer on people basic rights that are immune from legislative abridgment and that would protect those areas of conduct that are particularly likely to be affected by the external preferences of others. Thus, some people are racists, while others hate to hear the expression of opinions they disapprove of. In the absence of some constraints on the power of the majority, such external preferences are likely to find expression in racist laws, or laws abridging freedom of speech. The solution is to confer rights to free speech and to the equal protection of the laws in a basic Bill of Rights. In this way Dworkin can neatly propose an answer to the question of what justifies the apparently undemocratic judicial review of legislation enacted by a democratic legislature.

One further problem with preference-utilitarianism may be noted at this point. Since a society tends to shape the preferences of its members, can it be argued that preference-utilitarianism fails to provide an independent critical standard by which the morality of a society's laws and institutions may be judged? Capitalism, for example, may be said to generate wants and preferences of a highly materialistic nature: preferences which might not exist in other types of society, such as a society of subsistence farmers. To judge capitalism in terms of the preferences it has itself created is inevitably to endorse it. (Caveat: perhaps this is not inevitable, since it can be argued that capitalism generates preferences that cannot be satisfied.)

This objection has an unfortunate tendency to portray individuals as the pliable objects of some force labelled "capitalism", or "society". We may also feel some scepticism about the claim that other societies are less acquisitive than capitalist societies: is not the difference rather that pre-capitalist societies provide few opportunities for regular and systematic acquisition and limitless accumulation? But the objection certainly points to an important range of problems. For will not people's preferences (whether external or personal) inevitably be tied up with their moral ideas and aspirations? Does that not mean that preference-utilitarianism judges a society by the values accepted in that society? If so, the theory is relativistic, and does indeed fail to provide an independent critical moral standard.

Utility and distribution

Questions of law and justice are quite commonly thought of as questions about how wealth, resources and opportunities should be distributed. Should the distribution of such things be *equal*? Or in accordance with *need*? Or with *merit*? One objection that is sometimes made to utilitarianism is that it shows no concern whatever with questions of distribution, and therefore cannot be an acceptable theory of justice, or an adequate guiding principle for the law.

It is quite true that the utilitarian is not concerned with how *welfare* is distributed: his concern is with the maximisation of welfare, with how much there is in total. If the utilitarian is faced with a choice between two societies in one of which welfare is equally distributed (or distributed according to need, or merit, depending on your favourite theory) and in the other of which gross inequalities of welfare exist, he will simply choose (as morally preferable) that society in which the sum total of welfare is higher.

To demonstrate this point clearly it is necessary to speak as if welfare could be quantified in a numerical fashion. Let us therefore imagine individuals as having so many "units of welfare" and let us compare the situations represented by the following two schemes:

Situation 1

Individuals:	A	B	C	D	E
Units of Welfare:	10	10	10	10	10

Situation 2

Individuals:	A	B	C	D	E
Units of Welfare:	2	2	2	2	95

In situation 1, everyone has an equal level of welfare, and the total level of welfare may be expressed as 50 units of welfare. In situation 2, by contrast, welfare is unequally distributed: E enjoys a very high level of welfare, whereas A, B, C, and D all have a comparatively low level. But the *total* level of welfare in situation 2 is 103, much higher than in situation 1. Being concerned to *maximise* welfare, a utilitarian will prefer situation 2 to situation 1. If we found ourselves in situation 1, and if it were possible somehow to move to situation 2, a utilitarian would advocate that change. This demonstrates two points about utilitarianism: that it is genuinely not concerned with the question of how welfare is distributed, but only with how much welfare there is in total; and, secondly, that utilitarians may sometimes have to advocate policies that would make many people, or even most people, worse off, if those policies will produce for others benefits which are large enough to *outweigh* the adverse effects.

However, it is a mistake to conclude that because the distribution of *welfare* does not concern him, the utilitarian is also not concerned with questions of how *wealth*, *resources*, and *opportunities* should be distributed. On the contrary, the utilitarian is not only concerned with such issues, but can argue that he alone has a convincing explanation of why we *should* be concerned with such issues. His basic argument is that a more equal distribution of opportunities, wealth and other resources is desirable because, and in so far as, it will maximise welfare. (For simplicity's sake I shall include wealth and opportunities under the general heading of "resources" in what follows.)

The utilitarian is provided with a good argument in favour of a more equal distribution of resources by the theory of diminishing marginal utility. Expressed very simply, this theory entails that an additional £1 given to a millionaire will make a negligible contribution to his welfare, whereas £1 given to a very poor man might be a significant contribution to his welfare, enabling him, say, to buy a meal that he could not otherwise afford. The £1 will therefore maximise welfare more effectively if placed in the hands of a poor man than if placed in the hands of the millionaire. If we aim to maximise welfare, we therefore have good reason to transfer resources from the rich to the poor.

If diminishing marginal utility were the only factor we needed to consider, the utilitarian would be a very strict egalitarian, believing in an equal distribution of resources, perhaps modified only to accommodate special needs. But there are other factors against which the argument from diminishing marginal utility must be balanced. For example, it is widely held that high productivity requires a structure of incentives to encourage people to work hard, to invest, and so forth. If this is true, it follows that strict equality of resources, by robbing individuals of strong and immediate incentives to work hard, will in the long run bring about a fall in productivity and an overall decline in welfare. Similarly it can be argued that the maintenance of an equal distribution of resources will require constant interference with the market on a scale that is unprecedented and that is bound to impair economic efficiency, thereby leading to a fall in welfare.

We are now in a position to see the strengths of the utilitarian attitude towards distributive issues. First, the utilitarian can claim that his theory explains the way in which we do in fact trade off equality against productivity and economic efficiency. This trade off is neither arbitrary nor hypocritical: it reflects the fact that the underlying concern is with the maximisation of welfare, that being a goal to which *both* redistribution and higher productivity can contribute. Secondly, the utilitarian can argue that he alone has offered a plausible explanation of why redistribution matters. When we take money from the rich and give it to the poor, he may argue, we do this because we believe it will *do more good* relieving poverty than being spent on trivial comforts. In holding that it will "do more good" we mean that the loss in welfare for the rich will be minimal but the gain in welfare for the poor will be substantial. What other reason for redistribution could there be? In particular, would anyone advocate equal distribution even when that reduced the general level of welfare? Going still further, we may ask whether anyone would advocate redistribution even when it made *everyone* worse off, including the poor?

It will be instructive to consider one type of theory that might advocate strict equality of resources even though this did reduce everyone's "welfare" judged in terms of utilitarian notions of happiness or preference-attainment. Suppose that someone argued that the central thing that matters from a moral point of view is life in a community of compassionate caring individuals who share everything and, in that sense, enjoy equality of resources. Life in such a community could be said to be the only existence worthy of a human being, and a value that is to be pursued even when it conflicts with the more impoverished utilitarian notions of welfare. It will be immediately seen that this theory is indeed egalitarian in a more radical way than is utilitarianism. But it is not, and could not purport to be, a *liberal theory*, since it works from a particular conception of the good which differs from utilitarian notions of preference-attainment (and, possibly, happiness) in that it has no sort of *neutrality* about it. A question worth considering (but too large to consider here) is that of whether any radically egalitarian theory can also espouse the ideas of liberalism.

Rules and utility

In the last section I said that, although the utilitarian is not concerned with equality of *welfare*, but only with the maximisation of welfare, he nevertheless has good reason to favour (within limits) a more equal distribution of *resources*. But the utilitarian's lack of concern with how welfare is distributed has a further implication that was not considered in the last section. Since he is only concerned with the overall maximisation of welfare, there is in principle no limit to the harm that the utilitarian will be prepared to inflict on individuals, provided that the harm is balanced by an even greater increase in welfare for others. Thus, it is argued, there is literally nothing that the utilitarian might not be prepared to do, given appropriate circumstances: killing the innocent, torture, lying, promise-breaking, might all in some circumstances be necessary if overall welfare is to be maximised. How can the utilitarian respond to this claim?

The most obvious line of defence would be to deny that torture, murder, and other such actions ever *would* actually maximise welfare. This defence raises questions (about the probable effects of actions in hypothetical situations) which are virtually impossible to answer. We may certainly say that the utilitarian has no grounds for *confidence* that the principle of utility would, in no circumstances, justify murder or torture. The utilitarian has a better defence in a more aggressive response, for he can plausibly argue that we would all (or nearly all) hold killing and torture to be right in circumstances where it clearly did maximise welfare overall. For example, in the Second World War, the fight against the Nazis may have required us to kill innocent persons in Germany and elsewhere. But we regard such killing as justified by the need to destroy an evil régime. Similarly, if a madman had hidden a nuclear device which was set to destroy the whole of South-East England at a pre-set time, we might feel justified in torturing him if this really was the only way of discovering the location of the bomb so as to defuse it. Thus the utilitarian will claim that we are all prepared to set aside our basic feelings of revulsion about such acts as torture when we are sure that welfare will be maximised most effectively by such an act.

34

But the opponent of utilitarianism may point out that these situations of the Second World War and the nuclear madman are cases where a catastrophe of immense proportions is threatened: in such cases, it might be argued, we should be prepared to set on one side our ordinary feelings about acts harmful to individuals. The utilitarian, however, must be prepared to do *anything* whenever such an act will increase welfare by however small a degree. Earlier in this chapter we described the utilitarian view of promises, and we need only remind the reader that the utilitarian will break a promise whenever he thinks it best on balance to do so.

The example of the promise points to a further problem. It can be argued that a society will maximise the welfare of its members only if those members do not themselves act upon the principle of utility. For example, it is in everyone's interests that there should be a developed commercial system, but this is possible only where people can rely on the promises of others. A society of utilitarians, it can be argued, will be a society where promises are frequently broken and cannot be relied upon: a society of utilitarians will therefore fail to maximise utility. To take another case, it might be in everyone's interests to have public gardens with beautiful lawns, but this will require everyone to refrain from walking on the grass. Now suppose that I am a utilitarian, I am alone in the garden, and am wondering whether I should walk on the grass. Walking on the grass will give me pleasure and will not affect the grass to any perceptible degree. Since I am alone, my act of walking on the grass will not encourage others to walk on the grass or make it more likely that they will do so. My act will benefit me and harm no-one: it will therefore maximise utility, and I will (as a utilitarian) decide to walk on the grass. If everyone is a utilitarian, everyone will, in similar circumstances decide likewise. Very soon the beautiful lawns will be damaged and scarred by footpaths marking popular short-cuts across the grass. Once again, a society of utilitarians will inevitably fail to maximise utility.

Various solutions to this problem can be offered by utilitarians. Bentham's answer was to emphasise the importance of *sanctions* for a utilitarian society: the promise-breaker and the grass-walker should be encouraged to keep their word and keep to the pavement by coercive penalties. A more popular answer significantly modifies the general utilitarian standpoint, and is usually called "rule-utilitarianism".

The rule-utilitarian holds that one should not decide upon individual actions directly by reference to the principle of utility. I should not ask myself whether breaking the promise or walking on the grass (or killing, or torturing) would have the best consequences overall. Rather I should regulate my actions by reference to *general rules*, these rules being themselves justified by reference to the principle of utility. Two versions of rule-utilitarianism may be distinguished for present purposes. "Ideal" rule-utilitarianism holds that I should regulate my actions by those rules that *would* maximise welfare *if* they were generally observed. "Actual" rule-utilitarianism holds that I should comply with those rules actually accepted and observed in my society, in so far as the general acceptance of the rules maximises utility.

There are many complex objections to rule-utilitarianism. I will briefly summarise three such objections. First, *ideal rule-utilitarianism* appears to be irrational in that it requires me to act as if something were the case when I know that it is *not* the case: observing the rule would maximise welfare *if* the rule were generally observed, but I know that it is *not* generally observed. Secondly, *actual rule-utilitarianism* is either conservative, or it fails to give one any determinate guidance: either we interpret it as requiring general compliance with accepted social rules, or as requiring such compliance only when the accepted rules are perfect from a utilitarian point of view. In the latter case, the theory fails to tell me what I should do when the actual rules are dis-utilitarian. Thirdly, all forms of rule-utilitarianism contain the following paradox: whilst presupposing that the whole point of the rules is a utilitarian one, they require one to comply with rules even where compliance will *not* maximise utility. If they *do not* require compliance in such circumstances, the theories do not differ from "act-utilitarianism" of the conventional type, which applies the principle of utility directly to individual acts.

Possibly the best society from a utilitarian point of view would be a society where rules are chosen by an elite group of utilitarians, but the bulk of the population remain un-enlightened non-utilitarians, who obey the rules without reflecting on the tendency of their actions to maximise or diminish welfare. This has aptly been described as "Government House utilitarianism". We tend to feel that such a society of manipulators and the manipulated would be profoundly objectionable, even if it did maximise welfare. But the question of why we have such feelings is a profound one on which you should reflect.

SELECTED READING

I. Probably the best introduction is:

J. J. C. SMART and B. WILLIAMS, *Utilitarianism: For and Against* (1973).

The classic texts are:

JEREMY BENTHAM, *An Introduction to the Principles of Morals and Legislation.*

J. S. MILL, *Utilitarianism.*

HENRY SIDGWICK, *The Methods of Ethics.*

II. Further reading:

DAVID LYONS, *Forms and Limits of Utilitarianism* (1965).

D. H. HODGSON, *Consequences of Utilitarianism* (1967).

D. H. REGAN, *Utilitarianism and Co-operation* (1980).

III. Theoretical problems of contract:

C. FRIED, *Contract as Promise* (1981).

P. S. ATIYAH, *Promises, Morals and Law* (1981).

NEIL MACCORMICK, *Legal Right and Social Democracy* (1982), Chap. 10 (also Chap. 11).

IV. Some of the reflections on practical reason contained in this chapter are loosely based on:

T. NAGEL, *The Possibility of Altruism* (1970).

2. Rawls

Introduction

John Rawls's massive book *A Theory of Justice* provides the most influential alternative to utilitarianism in present day jurisprudence and political theory. Rich in themes and densely packed with argument, the character of the book cannot be conveyed in a single expository chapter such as this. But I will endeavour to trace the major themes and issues in a way that will assist the reader in his efforts to study the book itself.

Rawls rejects utilitarianism on two main grounds. Utilitarianism, he argues, ignores the distinctness of persons, and it defines the right in terms of the good. These criticisms may be explained as follows.

1. Ignoring the distinctness of persons

When we are making decisions about our own welfare, we consider it rational to make short-term sacrifices in order to achieve long term gains. We suffer the dentist in order to get rid of the toothache, for example. Utilitarianism extends this form of decision-making to decisions concerning the welfare of society as a whole. The principle of utility rests on the assumption that, just as rationality requires us to make small sacrifices for larger gains, so it requires us to trade-off the welfare of some against the welfare of others. Just as the pain of a visit to the dentist may be justified by the increase of welfare resulting from the removal of the aching tooth, so the pain inflicted on one section of the population may be outweighed by the happiness accruing to the remainder. Thus, in order to decide whether (for example) slavery was morally justified in a particular society, the utilitarian would have to weigh the hardship inflicted on the slaves against the happiness accruing to the slave owners.

39

It is precisely this feature of utilitarianism, this willingness to make "trade-offs" in welfare, that most fundamentally seems to conflict with our moral intuitions. For, whether or not the utilitarian is ultimately led to condemn slavery, his *reasons* for condemning it appear to be misguided. It seems wrong to take account of the happiness enjoyed by the slave owners. Yet, for the utilitarian, if slavery is wrong it is wrong because that happiness is not sufficiently great to outweigh the suffering of the slaves.

Utilitarianism goes astray here in simply extending to society as a whole the principle of rational decision for individuals. When I go to the dentist, the pain that *I* suffer at his hands is outweighed by the pleasure that results from the cessation of *my* toothache. But the pain of slavery and the pleasures of slave ownership are experienced by *different* individuals, and there is no reason why the same principle should apply to decisions which must adjudicate between different individuals. Utilitarianism ultimately treats people as lacking any distinctness, but as receptacles in which welfare is to be maximised with the greatest possible efficiency.

2. The right and the good

Utilitarianism defines the right in terms of the good. That is, it begins with an account of what states of affairs are valuable or desirable and defines right action as action that leads to such valuable states of affairs. Classical utilitarians count happiness as the thing that ultimately matters, and regard an action as morally right or wrong according to its tendency to increase or diminish happiness. We have already seen that this approach has anomalous features: it requires us, for example, to take account of the happiness accruing to slave owners as a positive factor tending to justify the institution of slavery. But we may feel that the slave owner's happiness should be ignored because it is *unjustly* obtained. This suggests that we can only say whether someone's happiness is a *good* thing after we have answered a question of justice. In Rawls's view, questions of justice are prior to questions about happiness and welfare in the sense that it is only when we know a desire or pleasure to be *just* that we can regard it as having any positive value: the pleasures of sadists, for example, would have no merit within Rawls's theory because of their conflict with principles of justice.

This points us to a deeper sense in which Rawls's theory treats "the right" as prior to "the good". Rawls wants to construct an account of the principles of justice that does not presuppose a particular conception of a good and worthwhile life. Rawls wishes to offer a theory that is, in a sense, neutral between different ideals and aspirations, differing personal ideas of what makes life valuable. The principles of justice represent a framework within which different individuals have a fair opportunity to pursue their own goals and values.

The basic idea of the theory

I observed in Chapter 1 that a powerful factor which has tended to support utilitarianism is the idea that rationality is a matter of choosing effective means to the attainment of given ends. This conception of rationality is implied by the general structure of utilitarian theory, particularly the way that the morally right action is defined in terms of its efficiency in the maximisation of good consequences. As we have seen, Rawls objects to the direct application of criteria of rational prudence to decisions about society as a whole. But he is aware that the instrumental conception of reason is a powerful and attractive one. He is conscious also of the desirability of basing his theory on widely shared assumptions, and the instrumental conception of reason undoubtedly represents a widely shared view of rationality. Rawls's theory can perhaps best be understood as an attempt to employ criteria of rational prudence in a manner consistent both with the distinctness of persons and with the priority of the right over the good.

Rawls asks us to imagine a group of rational individuals who have to agree on a set of principles that will govern the basic structure and institutions of their society. They are to choose these principles on grounds of rational self-interest and in the knowledge that the principles chosen will be binding upon them. But their choice is constrained by the fact that they are deprived of certain types of knowledge about themselves: they are to choose, as Rawls puts it, from behind a "veil of ignorance".

Essentially, the veil of ignorance excludes knowledge of all those features that distinguish one person from another. Thus the rational persons in the "original position" (as Rawls calls the basic choice situation) do not know their own identities; they do not know what they do for a living, nor how intelligent they are, nor what their abilities might be; most importantly, although the persons know that they *have* a personal conception of the good life (and that it may differ from the conceptions held by others) they do not know what their own conception of a good life *is*, nor what their personal ideals and values may be.

Rawls believes that the veil of ignorance represents a set of conditions that it is fair to impose upon the choice of principles of justice. When we argue for this or that moral principle we regard it as proper to set on one side our personal interests and to judge the matter from a more impartial point of view. Utilitarianism achieves this impartiality by attaching equal weight to the welfare of each person. Rawls seeks to achieve it by erasing from the discussion all knowledge of features that distinguish one person from another. The veil of ignorance also attempts to ensure that Rawls's theory of justice will be neutral between different conceptions of the good. Since the persons in the original position do not know what their own conception of the good is, they will choose principles that do not seek to reflect or embody any one particular conception, but that provide a framework within which the pursuit of differing ideals is possible.

The rational persons in the original position will choose (Rawls argues) two principles of justice, that we may formulate as follows (simplifying slightly):

> The first principle holds that each person is entitled to the most extensive system of basic liberties that is compatible with a similar system for everyone else.
> The second principle holds that social and economic inequalities are only fair so far as they work to the advantage of the least advantaged people in society.

The first principle takes priority over the second in that it is only when the first principle is completely satisfied that we can apply the second principle at all. The meaning of the two principles will become clear as we discuss them in detail.

The difference principle

"The difference principle" is the name that Rawls gives to the second principle of justice as I have formulated it above. The principle requires that inequalities in the distribution of resources must be justified by reference to the interests of the least well-off. Thus managing directors generally earn more money than car park attendants. This disparity in earnings is justified, in Rawls's view, only if a drop in the earnings of managing directors would make car park attendants less well-off than they are at present. This might be the result if, say, high earnings were necessary to attract able people into managing directorships and a fall in their earnings would result in a loss of management talent, a decline in efficiency, and a corresponding decline in the economy making everyone (including car park attendants) worse off. Rawls is prepared to allow a trade-off between economic efficiency and strict distributive equality in a rather similar way to the utilitarian. The difference is that, whereas the utilitarian will allow differential earnings and incentives in order to increase the general or overall welfare, Rawls will allow such inequalities only when they are necessary to increase the welfare of *the least advantaged*.

Rawls's reasons for favouring the difference principle are best understood by contrasting the principle with rival liberal conceptions of justice. Rawls contrasts the principle with what he calls the "system of natural liberty", and with the notion of equal opportunity. The system of natural liberty is essentially the pure free market with no redistribution of wealth through taxation and so forth. Rawls believes that we would find such a system objectionable because it allows people's prospects to be unduly influenced by factors which are irrelevant from a moral point of view, such as whether their parents are rich. We might then be tempted by the idea of equality of opportunity. This conception of justice seeks to ensure that people's prospects are determined by their natural talents and the amount of effort they put in to using those talents: their prospects should not be determined by the accident of social class and fortune. But, Rawls argues, this position, though superficially attractive and very influential, is unstable. For, once we have come to regard social class and fortune as arbitrary factors that are irrelevant from the point of view of justice, we can have no good reason for not regarding natural talents and abilities in exactly the same light. We no more *deserve* our talents and abilities than we deserve our parents' fortune: both are equally irrelevant from the point of view of justice. Accordingly, it is just as wrong for a person's prospects to be determined by his talents and abilities as it is for his prospects to be determined by his parents' wealth.

The difference principle embodies this view of natural talents in the following way. If I am a talented individual in a Rawlsian society, I will be allowed to increase my material welfare only if, in doing so, I also increase the material welfare of the least advantaged. Thus my talents are not resources that I may exploit for my own benefit alone: they are to be regarded as common assets that must be exploited for the benefit of everyone.

According to Rawls, rational persons in the original position would choose the difference principle as a basic principle of justice to regulate their society. They would choose this principle, in preference to other alternatives such as the principle of utility, because they would base their choice on very conservative and cautious criteria of rational decision. From behind the veil of ignorance, the rational persons are faced with a very difficult problem. They must choose principles of justice which will regulate the basic structure of their society, and so will fundamentally affect their own prospects in life, the resources and liberty that they will enjoy. But they do not know the position that they will occupy in such a society, nor do they have enough information to form a meaningful estimate of how probable it is that they will be among the better-off or the less well-off. Given the seriousness of the choice and the paucity of information on which the choice must be based, the rational persons will make their decisions according to the "maximin" rule. The maximin rule holds that alternative options should be ranked in terms of their *worst* outcomes. Imagine, for example, that I am trying to decide whether I should become a civil servant or a bank robber, and assume that my one concern is with how much money I will acquire in my chosen profession. If I am a very successful bank robber I might make £100,000 per annum (the best outcome), but if I am an unsuccessful bank robber I might make nothing (the worst outcome). If I am a civil servant I might be promoted to a job where I earn £20,000 per annum (the best outcome), or I might remain on a salary of £5,000 (the worst outcome). If I choose according to the maximin rule I will choose to be a civil servant, since I will rank the alternative occupations by their worst outcomes, and being a civil servant has the best worst outcome.

It is not difficult to see how the maximin rule would lead to the choice of the difference principle in preference to the principle of utility. Under either principle. the best outcome would be finding that I am in the most advantaged group in society, and the worst outcome would be finding that I am in the least advantaged group. Now, since the difference principle permits increases in overall welfare only when these benefit the least advantaged group, it is necessarily true that (in these two alternatives) the difference principle is most favourable to the interests of the least advantaged group. It therefore has the best worst outcome (and satisfies maximin) from the point of view of the original position. If, when the veil of ignorance is lifted, I discover that I am one of the least advantaged persons, I can rest assured that everyone will be labouring for my benefit, since the difference principle will permit other people to improve their material welfare only if, in doing so, they also benefit me. Under the principle of utility, on the other hand, my prospects would be more uncertain: they would be required to benefit me only if that was the most efficient way of increasing overall welfare, and it is conceivable that an increase in overall welfare might best be achieved by *sacrificing* my interests and making me worse off (*e.g.* by enslaving me).

We may agree with Rawls that *if* the choice is made according to maximin, the principle chosen would be the difference principle. But choice according to maximin only has a claim to rationality so long as we are ignorant of the various probabilities. In the choice between bank robbery and civil service, it would be irrational to choose according to maximin in circumstances where I know that as a bank robber I am virtually certain to make £100,000 per annum, and that as a civil servant it is most improbable that I will make more than £5,000. Rawls does not allow his persons in the original position sufficient knowledge to form an estimate of probabilities: but is he justified in so restricting their knowledge? After all, such a restriction does not seem necessary in order to secure the impartiality and fairness that we feel should characterise the choice of principles of justice, since the knowledge of probabilities would be the same for everyone and equally available to everyone. Moreover, the utilitarian regards it as an important part of his case to argue that the principle of utility is in fact *most unlikely* to lead to the justification of institutions such as slavery: but Rawls's exclusion of probabilities has the effect of disallowing all such appeals to the probable results of applying different principles.

In fact, Rawls adjusts the conditions of the veil of ignorance in order to ensure that the principles which are chosen as a result are the two principles that he wishes to argue for. This is not a flaw in his theory, or an intellectual sleight of hand. Rather, as we shall see later in this chapter, it reflects the fact that the original position and the veil of ignorance are not intended to *justify* the two principles of justice so much as to elucidate their deep philosophical presuppositions. The two principles do not require justification since, in some sense, we already intuitively accept them.

The intuitive appeal of the difference principle may be doubted, however. Rawls argues that the arbitrary nature of the natural distribution of talents should lead us to regard talents and abilities as resources to be exploited for the benefit of everyone. But, as Robert Nozick said, why should the same argument not be applied to bodily organs? After all, some people have two healthy kidneys and two eyes and others do not. This difference is not *deserved*, but is arbitrary from a moral point of view. So why should kidneys and eyes not be regarded as common resources? Why not parallel the coercive redistribution of wealth with a coercive redistribution of eyes and kidneys? In fact to regard either abilities or organs as common resources appears to give persons rights *in other persons*. What could be a more direct violation of the distinctness of persons than that? Yet it was precisely on the ground that it ignored the distinctness of persons that Rawls rejected utilitarianism. Nozick argues that, if we take seriously the idea of the moral distinctness of persons, we will reject the notion that some persons have a right to be benefited by others.

A different type of objection to Rawls's difference principle comes from a radical egalitarian standpoint. The difference principle could permit a considerable degree of inequality when this inequality works to the material benefit of the least advantaged, in the sense of providing the least advantaged with more "social primary goods" than they would have in the absence of the inequality. "Social primary goods" include liberty, opportunity, wealth and self-respect. The radical egalitarian will claim that inequality is in itself such a distorting and damaging feature of social life that it ought not to be tolerated even when the elimination of equality will make everyone (including the least advantaged) worse off.

Rawls might reply to this type of attack by developing the idea that self-respect is itself one of the social primary goods in terms of which the welfare of the least advantaged is to be assessed. But let us put that line of defence on one side for the moment. Rather, let us ask what makes equality such an important value that it is to be pursued even to the point of making everyone worse off (this should remind us of the discussion in Chapter 1 about whether there can be any non-utilitarian reasons for a concern with equality). The radical egalitarian might reply by saying that the form of human life which is truly valuable is one based on love, compassion, and mutual respect. Such a life, he might argue, is possible only in a community of complete equals. The value of such a life, and the consequent need for such a community, transcends in importance any concern with improved material welfare.

It is now possible to see why the liberal should reject such a radical egalitarian argument. The liberal seeks an account of justice as a framework within which people have an opportunity to pursue *their own* conception of a good and valuable life. But the radical egalitarian case (as I have described it here) rests upon *one particular* conception of the good life. It begins by asserting one way of life to be valuable, and then erects a political theory on that basis. But persons are capable of formulating and pursuing differing conceptions of a good life, and the liberal believes that justice is essentially concerned with the inviolability of that capacity.

Yet there are grounds for questioning the extent to which Rawls's own theory achieves this liberal ideal of impartiality between rival conceptions of the good. For how does Rawls justify his choice of "social primary goods" as the criteria by reference to which the welfare of the least advantaged group is to be evaluated? Rawls relies at this point on what he calls "the thin theory of the good". This theory holds that there are certain things (the social primary goods) which it is rational to want whatever else one may want, because of the role that they can play in the pursuit of any particular conception of the good. Liberty and money are obvious examples of things that will help me to carry out (or will not hinder) any plan of life that I may have in mind. Persons in the original position, having no knowledge of their personal conceptions of the good life, will therefore seek these "neutral" goods such as liberty and money.

The objection to Rawls's argument at this point is that the "thin theory of the good" is inherently biased in favour of bourgeois, individualist conceptions of the good life. Liberty and money are important constituents of the good life for an acquisitive middle-class American, but play a much less central part in a conception of the good life as life in a community of caring and compassionate equals. The neutrality between conceptions of the good, claimed to be a central feature of liberalism, is thus shown to be (it is argued) an illusion disguising a fundamental commitment to the acquistive values of capitalism.

This argument looks impressive at first glance, but becomes less formidable on closer examination. As I pointed out in Chapter 1, the legal order of a liberal society cannot claim to be neutral in the sense of allowing everyone to pursue his or her own conception of the good life, for what would we say of the conception of the good pursued by a psychopathic killer? The neutrality of a liberal legal order is based on the fact that the restrictions it imposes are justified, not by reference to one conception of the good being correct and another being incorrect, but by reference to the tendency of certain activities to interfere with the equal capacity of persons to pursue their own lives. This explains why liberalism will tend to favour individualistic (and possibly acquisitive) personal values. The man who wishes to pursue life in a certain type of community has preferences that extend to the behaviour of other persons. In a liberal society, he will be able to satisfy these preferences only with the consent of those persons. The man with purely acquisitive values has preferences that relate solely to what he *gets* and not at all to how other people behave. The man with materialistic goals is in a better position here, for he does not depend in the same way on other people sharing his idea of a good life.

The first principle of justice

Rawls's first principle of justice might at first sight be mistaken for the classic liberal principle that liberty may be restricted only in order to maintain equal liberty. This classic principle of equal liberty holds that the law is justified in interfering with conduct only when that conduct threatens the liberty of other persons: the sole aim of the law must be to maintain equal liberty. Rawls's first principle of justice is considerably less stringent, for his theory as a whole is not exclusively concerned with the value of liberty, but (in the second principle) with the value of equality as well. If the first principle of justice really corresponded to the classic principle of equal liberty, there would never be any scope for the application of the second principle.

The first principle takes priority over the second, in the sense that we may only set about rectifying inequalities in accordance with the second principle when the first principle has been completely satisfied. Now any rectification of inequality by the compulsory redistribution of wealth involves an interference with liberty: namely, the liberty to retain one's property. If the first principle protected *all* forms of liberty it would protect *this* liberty, giving it priority over the redistributive concerns of the second principle. The result would be that the compulsory redistribution of wealth to foster greater equality could never be justified. Since Rawls clearly does contemplate the compulsory redistribution of wealth, he cannot intend his first principle as a defence of liberty in general.

The first principle of justice differs from the classic liberal principle in that it protects, not liberty in general, but *certain specific liberties*. These are the conventional civil liberties of freedom of speech, freedom from arbitrary arrest, freedom of conscience and freedom to hold personal property. Such liberties cannot, in Rawls's view, justifiably be interfered with even where this would make for greater equality: it is in this sense that the first principle takes priority over the second.

Rawls's rational persons would attach this great importance to basic liberties because they must choose the principle of justice without knowing their own conception of the good. They know that they *have* such a conception, and that its pursuit will be very important to them, and that their conception may differ from that held by others in their society. In these circumstances the only safe thing to do is choose a principle which gives strong protection to liberty, thereby protecting the individual from the intrusive and oppressive effects of the disapproval that others may feel for our own idea of a good life. It is in this way that Rawls seeks to make his account of justice and right *prior* to an account of the good.

But, we may ask, why should the rational persons in the original position regard some liberties as more important than others? Taxation, for example, interferes with a person's liberty to dispose of his property as he chooses: in order to pay my employee £10,000 I may also have to pay the Inland Revenue £3,000; in order to give my friend a large sum of money I may have to pay capital transfer tax to the Inland Revenue; I am not free simply to give people what I like, without restriction. Now, why should people in the original position value freedom of speech so highly, but not freedom to dispose of their property? What justifies Rawls's choice of just *those* basic liberties? One cannot help suspecting that the only answer would have to be in terms of Rawls's own conception of a good and worthwhile life. Rawls assumes that a life of public concern and participation is superior to a life of material acquisition. But in making that assumption he sacrifices his claim to have offered a theory of justice as *prior to* particular conceptions of the good.

This poses a problem for modern liberals. It is ordinarily assumed that liberalism is consistent with a concern for equality and the redistribution of wealth. But the argument to this point suggests that any redistribution of wealth involves a discrimination between different aspects of liberty that is itself incompatible with the liberal ideal. Further light will be cast on this problem in the following chapter.

Reflective equilibrium

As we have seen, Rawls's theory describes a hypothetical situation in which rational persons would agree to certain principles. But why should this situation and this agreement have a bearing on *us*? After all we are not in the original position and have not agreed to the two principles of justice: so how does a description of circumstances in which we *would* have agreed to them demonstrate that they are indeed binding principles?

One answer to this question has been offered by Ronald Dworkin. Dworkin argues that Rawls's theory presupposes the existence of a basic right to equal concern and respect. When the fundamental laws and institutions of a society are being decided upon, the decision should show equal concern and respect for everyone. The device of the original position is a way of bringing this basic moral right to bear on concrete political issues: it enables us to say what the result of a decision showing equal concern and respect would be.

Dworkin's view is a revealing and stimulating one. But it is doubtful if it can do enough to cast light on the peculiar features of the veil of ignorance. After all, is it not arguable that equal concern and respect should be for persons as they are actually constituted, with all of their peculiar talents and characteristics? But the veil of ignorance excludes from the decision all knowledge of features that distinguish one man from another.

An alternative explanation of the significance of Rawls's original position denies that the argument is meant as a strong *justification* of the two principles of justice. Indeed, if we assume that justice is not reducible to some further question of utility, it is hard to see what a justification of the fundamental principles of justice could be. Rather than a *justification* we should look for an *explanation*: an account of what it is about *us* that makes *those* the principles of justice that we accept.

Rawls places considerable weight on the idea of reflective equilibrium. He holds that the two principles of justice should reflect our moral judgments when considered in reflective equilibrium. The meaning of this is best explained by means of an example. Suppose that I asked you for your moral views about a range of issues concerning the taking of human life: abortion, euthanasia, capital punishment, killing in self-defence, killing in defence of property, killing soldiers in war, killing enemy civilians in war, etc. Having ascertained your opinion on these matters, I then ask you what coherent set of principles would serve to justify *that* set of moral judgments. It is unlikely that your initial moral judgments would correspond to any coherent principles that were morally appealing and did not draw arbitrary distinctions (this is because we rarely think of the various issues as related, although they clearly must be). You would then be faced with a choice. It would be necessary for you to abandon some of your original moral judgments, but you could choose which ones to abandon. By altering your original view about abortion (for example) you might be able to subsume all your judgments under one set of principles. By sticking to your views on abortion and altering your views on capital punishment you might produce another coherent set. All the time you would be seeking to achieve a coherent set of moral judgments that you were prepared to live by and that could be justified by reference to attractive moral principles. When you had achieved this happy state you could offer an account of your moral judgments as "considered in reflective equilibrium".

Rawls claims that if we go through this process in relation to our intuitive judgments about social justice (liberty, the distribution of resources, etc.) we will find that the two principles of justice are the closest approximation to our intuitive moral judgments considered in reflective equilibrium. Suppose that this is true, and that Rawls has indeed executed this remarkable feat. Still, most of the *philosophical* questions still remain to be answered. For what is it about us that makes *these* the principles of justice that we accept? What is it about us that matters from the point of view of justice?

One of the most fruitful ways of reading Rawls's account of the original position and the veil of ignorance is as an answer to these latter questions. The veil of ignorance in effect strips bare the moral persona: the rational persons in the original position lack knowledge of all those characteristics which distinguish one man from another and possess knowledge of only those characteristics which matter fundamentally from the point of view of justice. By demonstrating that the conditions of the original position would lead to choice of the principles that, in some sense, we already intuitively accept, Rawls describes the features that make justice a part of our moral life. Persons in the original position show the capacity to choose and pursue a personal conception of the good life, and it is this capacity that is the foundation of our concern with justice.

SELECTED READING

J. RAWLS, *A Theory of Justice* (1972) (at pp. viii–ix Rawls offers advice on how to abridge one's reading of this massive book).

N. DANIELS (Ed.), *Reading Rawls* (1975): an extremely valuable collection of articles on Rawls.

R. P. WOLFF, *Understanding Rawls* (1977).

BRIAN BARRY, *The Liberal Theory of Justice* (1973).

NEIL MACCORMICK, "Justice According to Rawls" (1973) 89 *Law Quarterly Review* 393: this article provides a helpful introduction to Rawls.

NEIL MACCORMICK, *Legal Right and Social Democracy* (1982), Chap. 5.

MICHAEL SANDEL, *Liberalism and the Limits of Justice* (1982).

R. DWORKIN, *Taking Rights Seriously* (1977), Chap. 6.

On the problem of the relationship between civil liberties, such as freedom of speech, and market liberties, such as freedom to dispose of property, see the discussion of Dworkin's theory of rights in Chapter 9.

3. Nozick, Markets and Justice

Popular political discussions very often assume that it is possible and desirable for the law to foster both liberty and equality. It is assumed that we can be made more free and that, at the same time, a more equal distribution of resources can be achieved. In fact one of the long-running disputes of modern political theory concerns the relationship between liberty and equality and the question of whether they are indeed compatible.

Robert Nozick, in his book *Anarchy, State and Utopia*, gives that question a negative answer. He argues that any attempt to maintain an equal or near equal distribution of resources will demand constant interference with liberty. He asks us to imagine that we have, at long last, been able to achieve an equal distribution of wealth and resources in our society. What will be the result? Inevitably people will begin trading and making contracts with each other. Very soon, their transactions will upset the originally equal distribution of wealth. If, for example, a very large number of people like to hear X sing, they may be prepared to pay a small sum to attend her concerts, or to purchase her records. The result will be that X soon has a lot more money than many other people who do not have such a fine singing voice, or other marketable talents. The transactions through which X makes this money are individually fair and freely entered into, but they have the effect of bringing about an unequal distribution of wealth. If we wish to maintain an equal distribution, we will have to interfere with such free and fair transactions.

It is not only the strict egalitarian who, in Nozick's view, will have to embark on such constant interference with liberty: the same applies to anyone who holds what Nozick calls a "patterned" conception of justice. A "patterned" conception of justice views justice as a matter of the pattern of distribution which is achieved. Thus "distribution according to need", "distribution according to intelligence", and "equal distribution", would all be patterned conceptions of justice: they judge the justice of a situation by where the resources end up. Against such conceptions of justice, Nozick presents a "historical entitlement" view of justice. According to this view, the justice of a distribution of goods should be assessed not by where the goods end up, but by how the distribution came about. If it came about entirely as a result of transactions which were freely entered into, and without the use of force or fraud, then it is a fair distribution.

Nozick does not present a fully developed version of the historical entitlement theory of justice. Rather, he tells us what the general features of such a theory would be. The theory would consist of three sets of principles: principles of acquisition, of transfer, and of rectification. Principles of acquisition determine the circumstances in which someone can acquire ownership of formerly unowned resources. Principles of transfer determine the way in which the ownership of resources may be transferred from one person to another. Principles of rectification determine what should be done to rectify a distribution that is *unjust* in terms of the first two principles, *e.g.* what should be done when property has been acquired by fraud.

So far we have seen only the argument that patterned conceptions of justice conflict with liberty in a way that historical conceptions do not. But what if someone thought that the sacrifice of liberty was justified? What reasons are there for preferring the historical entitlement view of justice to its patterned rivals?

First of all we may note a sort of paradox that the patterned view of justice finds itself involved in. Suppose that we believe in equal distribution. We will then consider Distribution 1 to be just, and Distribution 2 to be unjust:

(Persons)	A	B	C	D	E	F
Distribution 1:	100	100	100	100	100	100
Distribution 2:	98	98	98	98	98	110

But Distribution 2 may have come about as the result of voluntary exchanges from the starting point of Distribution 1. If Distribution 1 was just, how can Distribution 2 be unjust? What acts of injustice are involved in the transition from 1 to 2?

Secondly, it seems hard to accept that anyone could really be tempted by patterned conceptions of justice, once we separate such conceptions from other related ideas, such as the prevalence of exploitation, or the need to relieve poverty. Suppose that A, B, C, D, E, and F are individuals each inhabiting his own desert island. By his strenuous efforts and skill, F has created a comfortable life for himself and has material possessions in greater abundance than have A, B, C, D and E, who lead much more austere lives. Does the inequality mean that A, B, C, D and E have a claim of justice against F? Can they demand a share of his possessions?

Artificial examples such as this help us to detach a pure concern with patterned conceptions of justice from the idea (for example) that workers in modern society are exploited and should *therefore* receive a greater share of wealth than they do through the market. Nozick would reject such notions of exploitation, but they are, just the same, ideas of historical justice rather than patterned distribution. We saw in Chapter 1 that it was difficult to imagine any non-utilitarian reason for a concern to equalise resources and we see the same problem repeated here. It is hard to comprehend anyone who simply insists that equal distribution matters in and of itself, and not as a means to the maximisation of utility, or as a way of rectifying the injustice of worker exploitation.

Theorists who subscribe to patterned conceptions of justice tend to envisage the problem of social justice in a particular way. They imagine that the total wealth of society can be regarded as a cake and the problem of justice can be seen as a question about how the cake is divided up. It is not surprising, in view of this approach, that equal distribution has strong supporters, with distribution according to need coming a close second. Some theories emphasise that the way the cake is distributed will affect the *size* of future cakes, while other theories play down this fact. In Nozick's view, the whole approach is misguided. There is no one who is entitled to treat society's total wealth as a cake to be divided up as we please. The wealth is brought into existence by individuals, and they already have rights attaching to it.

At this point we must consider Nozick's account of individual rights. It is a basic assumption of Nozick's theory that all persons have rights. These rights must not be violated: they operate as side-constraints on what we do, in the sense that, whatever we do in the pursuit of our own aims, we must not violate the rights of others. Now it is frequently asserted that Nozick's choice of basic rights is arbitrary. He says that we have rights to liberty and property, but there is no reason (it is argued) why we should pick on just *those* rights. Why not, for example, say that people have a right to welfare? Since a different choice of rights would remove the whole basis of Nozick's theory, this is a very serious criticism. It is, nevertheless, quite misguided.

The basis of Nozick's theory of rights is the idea of the distinctness of persons. We have seen that Rawls criticises utilitarianism for ignoring the distinctness of persons. Nozick takes this notion to involve the idea that each person has exclusive rights *in himself*, and no rights in other persons. This implies the existence of rights to liberty (since no one may interfere with others except to prevent their interference with him, etc.) and rights to property. Property rights are the result of the rights that I have in my own labour. Having exclusive rights in my own person, I have rights in my own labour. If I mix my labour with any object that is at present not owned by anyone, I acquire a right to that object. Having acquired an exclusive right to the object, I can transfer it to anyone that I choose. Thus the basic features of the historical entitlement theory of justice are built directly on the notion of the distinctness of persons.

Nozick's choice of rights is not arbitrary. If he had included among them a right to welfare (for example) he would have been negating the entire basis of the theory. A right to welfare (understood as entailing a duty on others to see that I receive some minimal level of welfare) would be a right to the assistance of other persons: it would be a right in the labour of other persons and thus would violate the distinctness of persons. Nozick accuses Rawls himself of ignoring the distinctness of persons, particularly in insisting that individual abilities should be regarded as resources to be exploited for the benefit of the least advantaged. Indeed, from this point of view, Rawls's theory scarcely seems superior to utilitarianism.

Even if we accept Nozick's starting point, however, it is doubtful if it leads to the conclusions he draws from it. The central difficulty concerns the argument that we can acquire the exclusive ownership of unowned objects by mixing our labour with them. Historically, this theory was put forward in the seventeenth century by John Locke, and in Locke's version it applied so long as there was "enough and as good" left over for other people. Nozick gives a sophisticated and rather tortuous modern version of this "Lockean proviso". But, in any case, why should one's labour give a right to the whole value of the object with which it is mixed? For example, oil and gas (being scarce resources) have an economic value while they are still in the sea bed. Before they can be utilised, however, they must be raised to the surface, and this involves labour. If I expend my labour in extracting the oil and gas, I am clearly entitled to the full value of my labour. But why should I be entitled to the full value of the oil and gas, including the value that they had simply as scarce resources and quite independently of my labour?

Nozick suggests that wealth should not be regarded as a big cake to be divided up: wealth is brought into existence by the efforts of individuals. But this is not true of *natural resources*: they simply exist and are not brought into existence by anyone. Of course, individual labour may be necessary before the resources can be *used*, but I am not denying that individuals are entitled to the value of labour expended. There is no reason why their labour should give them an exclusive right in resources that they did not produce (except from a utilitarian point of view, where such a right in resources might be offered as an incentive to useful effort). Thus it may be that Nozick's argument goes astray at this point and that, from his basic premises, he should have reached different conclusions. Perhaps he should advocate something like a resources tax which would tax people on the basis of the quantity of natural resources that they are consuming. The proceeds of such a tax might be distributed equally, on the basis that no one can have a better right than anyone else to natural resources. Indeed, redistribution should operate globally, with the developed world compensating the undeveloped world for their consumption of resources to which the undeveloped world is equally entitled.

There is a problem with the above argument, however. I have argued so far that a person may have an absolute right to his labour and to the value that his labour has added to an object, but not an absolute right to the whole object. This is because natural resources are not brought into existence by anyone, and there is no reason why any person should have a greater right to them than another person. But if this argument applies to natural resources, would it not also apply to natural talents and abilities? They are not possessed by an individual as a result of any labour on his part, but are the result of a natural distribution which is arbitrary from a moral point of view. And is this not Rawls's point in arguing that natural talents and abilities should be regarded as resources to be exploited for the benefit of people generally, and not just for the benefit of the person who possesses the talent or ability?

The correct response to this argument must be that our basic premise is the distinctness of persons, and the idea that personal abilities are common resources directly contradicts that premise. It is surely possible to draw a distinction between those things which are part of or an aspect of the person, and those things that the person possesses "externally": things that he uses but which are not part *of* him. Natural resources would fall into the latter category and natural abilities into the former. The basic idea of an exclusive right in oneself and in one's labour is itself a right in something that one has not brought into existence. An exclusive right in one's labour must necessarily entail an exclusive right in one's own ability; but, as we have seen, it does not entail an unrestricted right to appropriate the whole value of natural resources.

Markets and equality

Is Nozick correct when he claims that market transactions will inevitably upset any patterned distribution, such as an equal distribution? So long as we focus our attention on money, and perhaps physical objects, Nozick's claim would seem to be obviously true. But there is no reason why an egalitarian should disregard other resources such as spare time, entertainment, and travel. Once we do take account of this wider range of "goods", transactions on the free market may very often be regarded as *preserving* rather than upsetting equality.

Suppose that, in a certain community, individuals all have an equal amount of money on January 1. On January 2 many of them attend pop concerts, theatres and football matches, paying a small admission price in order to do so. The result is that the pop stars, theatre companies and football clubs have more money and the audiences have less money than they had on January 1. An inequality of monetary wealth has been produced. Should an egalitarian set about rectifying this inequality by redistributing the money? Before he does so, he should reflect that the people who attended the concerts, shows and football matches must have considered the opportunity of attending to be worth the admission price: otherwise they would not have gone. So, in terms of their own evaluations, they were no worse off (except in purely monetary terms) as a result of attending. If we make the highly artificial assumption of perfect competition in the market, we can also say that the admission price for each is based on the lowest margin of profit for which the performers will be prepared to perform: if the price was any lower, no shows and matches would take place. *On these assumptions* it can be seen that any redistribution of money would not *rectify* an inequality but *produce* one. The audiences would have had the benefit of the entertainment, *and* would get their money (which they were happy to spend) returned. The performers, who were prepared to work only for a financial return of a certain size, will have laboured without reward.

The example proceeds on the basis of very simplistic and unrealistic assumptions. Nevertheless, it should demonstrate the point that mere differences in monetary wealth do not always represent inequality in resources or in welfare: to rectify a monetary inequality can be to produce an inequality at the more fundamental level of resources or welfare (we need not, for present purposes, develop the latter distinction between resources and welfare). If for example I like fast cars and lots of cash and am prepared to work for it, and you like lots of spare time and are prepared to make do with less money, the difference in our incomes is likely to reflect differing tastes, rather than anything else. We may both be getting what we want out of life; we may both have an equally high level of welfare, if that is judged in terms of how far we are getting what we want; and, if leisure time may be regarded as a resource, we may have equal resources, since my greater income will be matched by your greater leisure. An egalitarian who focuses solely on money and sets about taxing me and benefiting you, is making us unequal. You are now getting the spare time *and* the money, while I am having to work hard to get the cash that I want, whilst also having to get the cash that benefits you.

Notice also that this crude monetary egalitarianism discriminates unfairly between different conceptions of a good life. The chap who likes leisure time and little money does very nicely thank you: the chap who likes money and fast cars has to work much harder than would otherwise be necessary.

Nevertheless, it is only within very narrow constraints and on rather artificial assumptions that the market can be regarded as equality-preserving. First because of the absence in the real world of perfect competition, the tendency towards monopoly, and so on. Secondly, because differences in monetary income do not always (or even largely) reflect differing preferences between, for example, leisure and cash: to a considerable extent they reflect the accident of social circumstance and differences in ability. Both of these factors, as Rawls emphasises, are arbitrary from a moral point of view. So there is no doubt that a concern with equality (of resources or of welfare) will demand extensive interference with market transactions and to that extent Nozick's objections to such "patterned" theories of justice are relevant. But we should be careful to note (on the other side of the coin) that the egalitarian has good reasons for being concerned to preserve the operation of the market, within limits. Only through the market can differing wants and preferences be co-ordinated, so that equal concern and respect for such differing wants demands preservation of free market transactions. Also, one of the values that frequently underlies egalitarianism (as the case of Rawls makes clear) is a concern with autonomy, understood as the capacity to formulate and pursue a personal conception of the good life. The free disposition of our property as we choose is, for many people, a major constituent of their idea of a good life, and such freedom should be accorded respect even if it has to be traded off against the demands of egalitarian redistribution.

It should be noted, in conclusion, that Rawls's own theory carefully provides for the operation, within limits, of market transactions. His two principles of justice are intended to apply only to what he calls the "basic structure" of society. By this he means the major institutions such as property rights, the constitution, the market and the family. Within the framework of the basic structure, particular distributions of wealth are not to be judged by reference to the two principles of justice, but by reference to criteria of *procedural* justice. The exact implications of this are far from clear, but it seems to represent an acknowledgment, by Rawls, that even a patterned theory of justice must respect the moral importance of market transactions.

Problems of private law

To a large extent, the law has traditionally been based on *historical* conceptions of justice. Whether or not a person should be held liable to pay damages in tort, for example, is conventionally regarded as dependent upon past facts: was the person negligent? did he allow some dangerous thing to escape from his land? etc. Liability in contract is regarded as hinging on the presence of an offer and an acceptance and the breach of a term that was expressly or implicitly agreed to. But in recent years this conception of the law has been challenged as unsound in principle, and as failing to reflect the realities of the law in practice. A more purposive, policy-oriented approach to the law has been emphasised, with the traditional legal doctrines being portrayed as a form of subterfuge that is employed to conceal the real basis for decision, or as a "technique" that is manipulated to serve policy goals.

More generally, it has been argued that, in the context of a redistributive welfare state, concerned to foster greater equality, the doctrinal basis of private law should be rethought. There is no reason, it is argued, why redistributive concerns should be limited to revenue law and welfare law: the law of contract and tort could themselves be developed along lines favourable to the egalitarian redistribution of wealth. For example, the law of tort may be regarded as a mechanism for placing the burden of social costs on those best able to bear them and best able to spread the loss amongst the community as a whole. It has also been suggested that the concern with promise as the basis of contract (and the idea of freedom of contract) that dominated the period in the nineteenth century when contract doctrines assumed their classical shape, is now inappropriate, given the values that underlie other areas of the legal system such as welfare law. These views can only be evaluated in the light of philosophical reflection on the value of equality and the historical conception of justice. As we have seen, an egalitarian may have good reason for attaching importance to freedom of contract and the market and for refusing to apply a patterned criteria of justice to every particular distribution. Rather, like Rawls, he may insist that inequality should be rectified at the level of the basic structure but that, within a generally just basic structure, the justice of particular distributions should be determined by procedural or historical considerations.

SELECTED READING

R. NOZICK, *Anarchy, State and Utopia* (1974) Chaps. 7 and 8.
J. PAUL, *Reading Nozick* (1981): a very useful collection of essays on Nozick.
G. A. COHEN, "Robert Nozick and Wilt Chamberlain: How Patterns Preserve Liberty" (1977) 11 *Erkenntnis* 5.
HILLEL STEINER, "The Natural Right to the Means of Production" (1977) 27 *Philosophical Quarterly* 41.

Some fascinating reflections on the connection between markets and egalitarianism will be found in:
R. DWORKIN "What is Equality?" (1981) *Philosophy and Public Affairs* 185, 283.

For an example of the bearing of these discussions on private law, see:

A. KRONMAN "Contract Law and Distributive Justice" (1980) 89 *Yale Law Journal* 472.

4. Finnis on Objective Goods

The various theories that we have examined so far all seek to offer an account of justice that is neutral between different conceptions of a valuable and worthwhile life. The classical political theories offered by the Greeks had treated the nature of the good life as a central and fundamental problem for politics; but modern liberal theories have tended to view justice, the law and the state as ideally constituting a framework within which individuals can pursue their own ideas of a good and worthwhile existence. This is even true of utilitarianism, for, although that theory defines the right in terms of the good, the central value of happiness or welfare is thought of as a catch-all value, sufficiently broad to cover virtually any goal or project that the individual might choose.

Historically, there can be little doubt that the Humean conception of reason has played an influential role in the emergence and continued vitality of liberalism. As we saw in Chapter 1, the Humean conception of reason holds that every reason for action is related to a desire that the actor has. Reason can only tell us how best to attain the object of our desires. Reason cannot tell us that we ought to desire this or that. In turning to the natural law theory of John Finnis we are studying a theory that rejects the Humean conception of reason and uses that rejection as the basis of an argument that is broadly Aristotelian in character. Like the classical writers, Finnis takes as his starting point the question of what constitutes a valuable and worthwhile life. Only having answered that question does he proceed to investigate the values of justice and law that have been central to modern liberalism.

Desires and objective goods

In the Humean conception of reason, "desires" are basic. Reason

63

can tell us how to attain our desires, but not what to desire; from the point of view of reason, one desire is as good as another.

But a desire is not a simple psychological fact. There are limits to what will count as an intelligible desire. Once we began to appreciate those limits, we see the weaknesses of the Humean approach.

Suppose that we met a man who announced that he wanted a saucer of mud. We would be puzzled by such a curious desire, and would no doubt want to know *why* he wanted a saucer of mud. "Oh, no reason", he might reply, "I just *want* a saucer of mud." "Well", we could ask, "are you *studying* mud? Do you want to carry out tests of some sort on the mud?" "No, I'm not interested in mud at all. In fact I find it rather boring." "Do you want to *use* the mud for something? To make mud pies, or to fill a hole in the wall?" "No, I've no use for it at all." "Do you find mud pleasing? Do you like the way the light gleams over its surface? Does its smell remind you of seaside holidays?" "No. I've already told you, I just *want* a saucer of mud. As David Hume has demonstrated, one desire is as good as another from the point of view of reason. No desire can be said to be *irrational* unless it depends on false factual beliefs, which mine does not. I just want a saucer of mud and that's all there is to it!"

Hume would have to argue here that a desire for a saucer of mud strikes us as odd simply because it is unusual. But we tend to feel that such a desire is not simply unusual: it is unintelligible. The questions that we ask about this strange desire are attempts to understand it; and the questions are in effect trying to discover what it is about mud that makes it *desirable*. What makes mud a *good* thing to have? The insistence that one just wants a saucer of mud for no particular reason is an attempt to detach the notion of *desire* from the ideas of being *good* and being *desirable*.

For anyone sympathetic to the Humean account, things count as good in so far as they are desired. But the example of the saucer of mud shows that a desire is unintelligible unless it is related to some objectively good characteristics of the thing desired. The Humean account treats the notion of "desire" as fundamental and as in need of no further explanation. But we can now see that desires only make sense by reference to a deeper and more fundamental notion: the idea of objective goods.

Finnis does not use the saucer of mud argument (which I have borrowed from G. E. M. Anscombe) but the argument represents the general strategy of his attack on the Humean conception. An account of practical reason must start, not from desires, but from *goods*; and, being good independently of desire, such goods will be *objective goods*.

Objective goods

It is most important to realise, at this stage, that when we talk about "goods" we do not mean "morally good". Objective goods are not moral values, but things which make life worthwhile; qualities which render activities and forms of life desirable; they are, in Finnis's words, "forms of human flourishing".

Finnis lists seven basic objective goods: these are life, knowledge, play, aesthetic experience, friendship (or sociability), practical reasonableness, and religion. These goods do not form a hierarchy and are all equally fundamental. They form the basis for Finnis's account of practical reason, and thus for his theory of justice, rights and law.

One traditional image of natural law theory sees it as attempting to deduce prescriptive conclusions from factual premises, especially premises about human nature. On this approach we might have expected Finnis to offer some descriptive account of human nature, and then to deduce his list of objective goods from that account. Such an argument would fall foul of the is/ought distinction which is forever associated with the name of David Hume. According to the is/ought argument, one cannot validly pass from purely descriptive premises to a prescriptive conclusion. Thus, from the premise "all men are sociable" one cannot conclude "you ought to seek society". No description of observable facts about human nature will in itself justify conclusions about right and wrong, good and bad, or what one ought to do.

Finnis maintains that his own argument does not violate the is/ought distinction. He does not deduce his objective goods from any descriptive account of human nature. His argument is quite different, and an altogether more subtle one.

Finnis claims that the objective goods are self-evident. It is self-evidently true that, for example, knowledge is better than ignorance. This does not mean that it is *obvious*, or that everyone agrees on the good of knowledge. Rather the objective goods are presupposed by anything that could count as an argument of practical reason. The theoretical inquiries of science presuppose certain principles of theoretical rationality; those principles cannot be demonstrated or *proved*, for they would be presupposed by anything that could count

65

as a proof. In just the same way one cannot demonstrate that friendship ought to be pursued: for goods such as friendship would be presupposed by any argument that sought to offer reasons for action. To offer someone a reason for action is always to show how the action is related to an objective good. It follows that one cannot offer reasons for pursuing the objective goods: anyone who cannot grasp the importance that such goods must have for his conduct is simply unreasonable.

In relation to the basic good of knowledge, Finnis offers an additional argument. He claims that the denial that knowledge is a basic good is self-refuting. If I deny that knowledge is good, I must nevertheless believe that my *denial* is worthwhile. In telling you that knowledge is not good, I must believe that *that* item of information (*i.e.* that knowledge is not good) is worth having. Thus in *denying* that knowledge is good I am also *assuming* that knowledge is good: my denial is therefore self-refuting.

It is doubtful if this argument is successful. In giving you this or that information I may be committed to the judgment that the information is worth having. But I am not committed to the judgment that knowledge is an objective good. I may hold that knowledge is valuable only *instrumentally*, when it helps us attain our other goals without wasted effort. I may consider it worth knowing that knowledge is not in itself an objective good because this will save wasted effort in the acquisition of useless knowledge. In assuming that this item of knowledge is (instrumentally) good I am not committed to the view that *all* knowledge is *in itself* good.

Goods and the common good

Even if we accept Finnis's claim that some list of objective goods must form the basis of our conceptions of practical reason, we may still refuse to regard the objective goods as the basis of *morality*. Suppose that knowledge, play and aesthetic experience are indeed good things that ought to be pursued or participated in. Nevertheless, we may argue, there is no reason why we should be concerned with the enjoyment of these goods by other people. We have reason to pursue these goods *for ourselves*, but not for others. Yet morality is distinguished from mere prudence by the fact that it is not limited to a concern for self-interest, but is based on generalised concern for others. So how can Finnis's objective goods provide the basis for a theory of *morality*?

One argument offered by Finnis relies on the notion that friendship is itself an objective good. It is good to have friends and one's life is impoverished if one has no friends. But having a friend is not simply a matter of enjoying someone's company or finding someone amusing. Friendship involves caring about the welfare of the other person for his or her own sake. Thus friendship is an objective good which leads us beyond an exclusive concern with ourselves. The complete egoist who regards all other persons as resources or means to his own satisfaction will lead an impoverished life because he will be incapable of friendship.

The political community is not a relationship between friends, but it is nevertheless analogous in some respects to friendship: both friendship and community are forms of the objective good of sociability. The realisation of this objective good therefore leads us beyond exclusive concern with ourselves and into a concern with community, or the "common good". Life in a community is itself a constituent of the good life (not merely a means to that end) which can be attained only by our concern for the common good.

Another basic good, according to Finnis, is the good of practical reasonableness. Practical reasonableness structures our pursuit of the other basic goods, requiring us (for example) to formulate a coherent plan of life which intelligently pursues the basic goods, or some range of them. One of the requirements of practical reasonableness is that there should be "no arbitrary preferences amongst persons". This involves accepting that the basic goods are capable of being pursued and enjoyed by any human being and that they are equally good when enjoyed by some other person as when enjoyed by myself. My own well-being is the first claim on my interest and reasonably so. But this is not because my well-being is more valuable than the well-being of some other person. Rather it is because my pursuit of my own well-being is the way in which I can best secure and realise the objective goods.

Finnis here faces a problem that confronts a number of other moral theories, such as utilitarianism. If the welfare of others matters just as much as my own welfare, should I not be *ridden* with moral concern for others? Should I not be constantly slaving away to improve the position of the poor, the sick, the starving, the underprivileged? But can the demands of morality really be *that* demanding?

One reply is "Yes, of course morality is that demanding. We really should live like that. Of course we all fall short of that ideal standard, but it nevertheless represents what we *ought* to do."

Underneath its appearance of moral stringency, however, this response actually embodies a slack and potentially vicious attitude to morality. For the response accepts too easily and too comfortably the idea of falling short of what morality requires. By happily conceding that morality says we *ought* to do all sorts of things that we never have done or will do, the response actually undermines the seriousness of morality itself.

Another reply seems to be offered by Finnis. Although the welfare of others matters just as much as your own welfare, you still have reasonable grounds for being mainly concerned with your own welfare. This is because looking after your own welfare is the most effective way of looking after welfare generally. The trouble with this reply is that it is probably false. It seems very likely that, by slaving away for the rest of my life to improve the lot of people in the Third World, I could make a greater contribution to human well-being than by anything else that I am actually likely to do. This would almost certainly do more for human flourishing generally than will a life exhibiting "reasonable self-preference".

Finnis's claim that the principle forbidding "arbitrary preferences amongst persons" is nevertheless consistent with "reasonable self-preference" depends in part on his denial of the possibility of utilitarian computations of overall welfare, with which I will deal later. But his argument also relies upon a distinctive and restricted notion of "the common good" which brings that notion much closer than we might have expected to liberal ideas of law and justice as a *framework* for the pursuit of individual projects.

For Finnis, the common good is a set of conditions which enables the members of a community to attain for themselves reasonable objectives. It is only given certain conditions (*e.g.* of stability, freedom, and order) that people can formulate and pursue their personal plans of life in accordance with the requirements of practical reasonableness. The common good (which for Finnis represents the central concern of law and justice) is the total set of conditions which makes such personal plans and projects a possibility.

This conception of the common good has a number of implications. First of all, it entails what Finnis calls the "principle of subsidiarity". This principle affirms that it is the proper function of a community to help individuals to help themselves, and to assist individuals in the pursuit of their projects. In turn, this means that Finnis's political theory is of a recognisably liberal cast: although his theory is based on a particular account of the good, it does not sanction the imposition of that conception on individuals. The purpose of the political community is to provide the essential pre-conditions for the exercise of reasonable choice by its citizens: its purpose is not to make the basic choices *for* citizens. Finally, Finnis's account of the common good leads to the conclusion that our moral concern for the common good need not be an obsessive concern with how well other people's lives are going, but is primarily a matter of fulfilling one's particular obligations in justice, performing con-tracts, and so on (see *Natural Law and Natural Rights*, p. 305).

This whole conception of the common good, with its broadly liberal implications, depends for its coherence on the idea that differing plans of life may be equally reasonable. If there was just one correct way of pursuing the various objective goods, then moral concern would require the enforcement of that one correct way as being "the common good". But there are diverse ways of combining and choosing between the objective goods, and the capacity of individuals to choose for themselves is itself (under the heading of "practical reasonableness") an objective good. But if knowledge, aesthetic enjoyment, friendship, play and the others are objectively good, how can I choose between them? If knowledge is a good, then I have reason to pursue knowledge, irrespective of what I want or choose: so how can I opt for a life that gives a low priority to the good of knowledge as against other values?

Finnis's answer to this question is that one must choose a coherent plan of life on the basis of one's capacities, circumstances, and tastes. Such a plan of life will involve concentration on some objective goods at the expense of others. Thus (to use Finnis's example) a scholar may have little taste for friendship, and may be completely committed to the search for knowledge: but it would be unreason-able for him to deny that friendship is a good in itself. It is one thing to have no taste for friendship, but it is "another thing, and stupid or arbitrary, to think or speak or act as if these were not real forms of good" (p. 105).

At this point, it can be argued, Finnis comes close to re-introducing elements of the Humean conception of practical reason. Hume holds that we have reason to pursue something (*e.g.* knowledge) only if we desire that thing, or if that thing will assist us in attaining our other desires. The *rejection* of the Humean view claims that knowledge (for example) is in itself *good*, and that that in itself gives us a reason to pursue knowledge. We should pursue knowledge because it is good, and not merely because, and in so far as, we desire it. Yet by introducing the notion of "taste", Finnis makes room for choice only by slipping a little bit of Hume between the action and the objective good. Friendship is an objective good, but the scholar has reason to pursue friendship only if he has a "taste" for it. Is this so different from saying that one has reason to pursue something only if you desire it?

The problem for Finnis is a fundamental one. How are we to explain the moral importance that attaches to freedom of choice? If there are certain objective goods, then surely what matters is the attainment of those goods. We can, of course, say that freedom of choice is itself a good, but that leaves unresolved the question of how far it should override the other goods. Should we respect people's freedom to choose things other than knowledge, friendship, aesthetic enjoyment, and so on? One way of explaining the importance of freedom of choice is by reference to a Humean theory that simply denies the existence of objective goods. Another way is to argue that the value of freedom forms part of a network of concepts (right, justice, legality) centring on the notion of respect for persons. The capacity of persons to formulate individual plans and projects is an important moral capacity that must be respected even when it is exercised misguidedly. The notion of respect for persons is, on this approach, independent of any questions about objective goods, desirable ways of life, and so on. Justice and rights are *prior* to questions about the good life. Such theories completely reject the attempt of Finnis to build a political theory directly on an account of objective goods.

Objective goods and utilitarianism

We have already examined one theory that places an account of the good at its starting point: utilitarianism. The utilitarian begins by affirming that pleasure, or welfare, or something of that sort, is good and ought to be maximised: the basic moral requirement is a requirement of maximising that good. Finnis's theory also begins with an account of good or goods. Should we therefore conclude that his theory is a form of utilitarianism, with a plurality of goods substituting for the good of "pleasure"?

The answer must be an emphatic "No". Finnis is careful to distinguish his theory from any form of utilitarianism and he offers a number of interesting arguments against the utilitarian position.

Finnis rejects the whole idea of maximising, which is central to utilitarianism. He claims that the various objective goods are incommensurable. By this he means that there is no common yardstick whereby they can all be measured: there is no way of saying how much knowledge (for example) would be "as good" as a certain amount of aesthetic enjoyment, or how much aesthetic enjoyment it would take to compensate for a loss of friendship. Because the various goods are incommensurable in this way, the injunction to maximise them simply makes no sense, just as it would make no sense "to try to sum up the quantity of the size of this page, the quantity of the number six, and the quantity of the mass of this book" (p. 115).

Finnis has an important point here. Nevertheless, we may legitimately wonder whether changes in the nature of social relations may not have had the effect of rendering the "goods" of friendship, knowledge, and so forth, commensurable by converting them into subordinate, instrumental, goods. If people came to experience their lives in such a way that friendship, learning, beauty, and the rest were evaluated simply as sources of enjoyment, these values would indeed have become commensurable (by ceasing to be independent values). One can argue that it is precisely because our lives have come to be experienced in this way that utilitarianism has been such a widely influential theory. Utilitarianism is too influential to rest on a mere intellectual error: it must reflect real features of our social life.

Because the objective goods are incommensurable, Finnis argues, one cannot "trade-off" one value against another. One cannot justify the killing of one person (for example) by the benefits (in terms of the objective goods) that will accrue to others as a result, because the calculations that would be necessary for such a trade-off to be possible are devoid of meaning. Thus, Finnis argues, one must not perform any act that in itself does nothing but harm a basic value. This is so even if that act will certainly have consequences that will promote or realize the objective goods. Suppose that a madman tells me that, unless I shoot an innocent person, he will shoot one hundred innocent persons. Even if I believe him and have good reason to think that, by shooting one person, I could save one hundred, I should not do the shooting. *My* act will merely be an act of killing, according to Finnis. Any good consequences that later follow will be realised as the result of *other* acts subsequent to mine.

This argument is a puzzling one. First because it presupposes that we have some way of individuating and describing actions independently of our moral judgments. But this is doubtful: if I shoot the innocent man, am I killing one person, or saving one hundred? Secondly, because not every situation of this kind will involve the problems of incommensurability that Finnis takes to be the fatal flaw in utilitarianism. When we are trading life for life (or one life for one hundred) no questions of incommensurability arise. Finnis wants to look at each action as completely discrete and self-contained, and he refuses to regard actions as elements in wider plans and strategies that must be evaluated as a whole.

Justice

According to Finnis, principles of justice are simply the concrete implications of the general requirement that one should foster the common good in one's community. The common good requires some degree of collaboration and co-ordination of conduct. This means that questions will arise about how the benefits and burdens of communal enterprises should be distributed. Should they be shared out equally, or according to needs and abilities, or according to "merit"? Also, there will be natural resources that are not the exclusive entitlement of any individual: a society must adopt principles governing the distribution of such natural resources, and governing access to, and rights in, communally owned property.

In addition to such problems of "distributive" justice, there will be problems of justice in the dealings between specific persons, *e.g.* the justice of keeping promises, or of compensating for injuries. Aristotle had called these matters questions of "corrective justice", but Finnis prefers the wider term used by Aquinas: "commutative justice".

Because Finnis sees the requirements of justice as simply a matter of fostering the common good, his account of justice is a flexible and pluralistic one. For example, he is not attracted by theories which offer a single principle to regulate all questions of distributive justice: distribute "according to need", or "distribute equally". Considerations of need have, according to Finnis, a certain priority, but other considerations are also very important. Considerations of desert, the functional requirements of one's role, and capacities (*e.g.* higher education for those capable of benefiting from it) are all relevant.

Some theorists draw a very fundamental contrast between distributive justice and commutative (or corrective) justice. On the one hand are theorists who give the central role to commutative justice. Justice for them is primarily a matter of property rights, the keeping of contracts, and the correcting (by punishment or by compensation) of injuries. Questions of *distributive* justice arise (on this view) only when the owner of some property wishes to distribute it, *e.g.* if I am considering how I should distribute my property amongst my children in making my will. Should I share it out equally, or according to need?

A rival approach gives the upper hand to distributive justice. Here the basic questions of justice concern how the benefits and burdens of social life should be distributed. Once a just distribution is achieved, any upset in the status quo (by theft, or injury, or breach of contract) must be rectified in order to restore the distributively just situation: this is the role of corrective (commutative) justice.

These rival approaches are well represented in the ranks of political theorists. For example, whereas Rawls adopts the latter approach, Nozick (with his insistence that the wealth of a society cannot be cut up like a big cake) is a good example of the former. But the approaches are also represented in the law, and in different ways of thinking about questions of contract and tort, for example.

On the theory which gives the principal role to commutative justice the main point about contract and tort must be that torts and breaches of contract are *wrong*. As wrongs they should be rectified, by the payment of compensation. The impact that such compensation will have on the way in which wealth is distributed generally is irrelevant.

But an increasingly influential way of thinking presents the basic question as one of distributive justice. In tort, for example, the main question is no longer thought to be one of who has *wronged* whom, but rather it is thought to be a question of who should bear certain risks and responsibilities. The mass production of consumer goods is an enterprise that benefits everyone but which, in various ways, is liable to harm unfortunate individuals. Who should bear the risk of such harm: the producer? the injured parties? everyone (*i.e.* should compensation to injured persons be paid from public revenues, financed out of taxation)? Instead of posing a question of how wrongs should be rectified (commutative justice) we can pose a question of how burdens should be distributed (distributive justice).

Finnis invites us to understand the nature of these debates by viewing the notions of distributive and commutative justice as labels adopted for convenience rather than as fundamentally different conceptions. They simply represent two different aspects of the general problem of fostering the common good. The basic question is always that of how the common good can best be served. When it is appropriate to think of people as engaged in a common enterprise, it may be appropriate to adopt the perspective of distributive justice. When people are not engaged in any common enterprise, their relationships are a matter of commutative justice. In the law of contract, for example, we may treat the parties as dealing with each other at arm's length, and this approach may encourage us to hold each contracting party strictly to the letter of his promises. But, from another point of view, a commercial contract can be seen as a kind of limited partnership, where the parties undertake shared risks. On the latter approach, when unforeseen circumstances occur which frustrate the common intentions of the parties, the resulting losses should be *shared*, rather than being borne by one party alone.

SELECTED READING

J. FINNIS, *Natural Law and Natural Rights* (1980).

Finnis's argument is developed further in:
J. FINNIS, *Fundamentals of Ethics* (1983). See also Finnis's essay "Scepticism, Self–Refutation, and the Good of Truth" in P. M. S. HACKER and J. RAZ (Eds.) *Law, Morality and Society* (1977).

The "saucer of mud" argument is borrowed from:
G. E. M. ANSCOMBE, *Intention* (2nd ed., 1963), pp. 70–72.

Part Two

Law

5. Hart

Legal positivism

Jurisprudence is often thought of as a long running battle between two camps: the "legal positivists" and the "natural lawyers". Both of these labels are crude distortions, concealing an enormous degree of complexity and diversity. But it is true that the debate about legal positivism has occupied a central place in jurisprudential debate for a long time. In studying Hart, we are turning to the work of the principal modern exponent of legal positivism, and some understanding of the general nature and characteristic claims of this position is essential.

Legal positivism emerged in its modern dress in the work of Jeremy Bentham and his disciple John Austin. Bentham mounted an assault on the forms of legal writing and reflection characteristic of the eighteenth century and epitomised by the writings of Sir William Blackstone. Legal writers such as Blackstone represented the law as enforcing natural rights. The systematic classifications they employed, and the principles they extracted, were based on a theory of natural rights. In this way, their expositions of the law become also attempted moral justifications of the law. According to Bentham this approach confused two quite different issues. On the one hand, the task of "expository jurisprudence" was to set out the existing law as it stood. On the other hand, the task of "censorial jurisprudence" was to subject the law to moral scrutiny, to expose its defects, and to propose reform. To expound the law as the expression and embodiment of natural rights was a dangerous conflation of two quite different enterprises. It was particularly objectionable, in Bentham's view, because the law should be criticised and evaluated by reference to the principle of utility and not by reference to a misguided belief in the existence of natural law or natural rights.

Another feature of traditional approaches to the law that

Bentham objected to was the tendency to treat law-making authority as a matter of moral or political legitimacy, appealing (in many cases) to a version of social contract theory as an explanation of the authority of the legislator to enact laws. Once again this confused factual issues about what the law *is* with moral issues about whether it ought to be obeyed. Law-making authority, like law itself, should be treated as a matter of social fact quite separate from questions of morality.

Bentham and Austin endeavoured to provide a firm foundation for the separation of expository and censorial jurisprudence by their general theories of law. Both Bentham and Austin treated law as a body of commands laid down by a supreme legislative body (called "the sovereign") in each legal system. Sovereignty was treated as a matter of social fact, consisting in the regular tendency of the bulk of the population to obey the commands of the sovereign.

Although profoundly critical of the legal theories offered by Bentham and Austin (indeed, Hart develops his own theory by exposing the flaws in Austin's), Hart shares with them the general aspiration to construct a positivist theory of law that distinguishes clearly between law and morals. We must therefore begin by explaining what this aspiration involves. At the end of this chapter, an ambiguity in the central claims of legal positivism will be pointed out.

The central claim of legal positivism is that law is separate and distinct from morality. This really involves at least two distinguishable ideas:

1. Positivists claim that we can work out what the existing law is without making any moral judgments. Whether some rule is a *legal* rule depends upon whether it has been laid down in some source such as a statute or a case. If it is to be found in some such source, a rule is a valid legal rule whether it is good or bad, just or unjust. Equally, the mere fact that a rule is a just and reasonable rule does not make it part of the law if it is not to be found in any recognised source of law.
2. Positivists claim that propositions of law, in which we state the existence of legal rights and duties, are not moral judgments. Opponents of positivism might argue that we cannot speak of a law as imposing duties and conferring rights unless we regard the law as morally binding. Positivists reply that such an

argument plays upon two different senses of the words "right" and "duty". Perhaps a law cannot confer *moral* rights and impose *moral* duties unless it is morally binding. But we can treat it as conferring *legal* rights and imposing *legal* duties whether or not we regard it as morally binding. Thus, positivists hold that *legal* rights and duties are not a variety of *moral* right or duty, but are quite diffferent.

It is all too easy to confuse these two positivist claims with a number of others, and we must note carefully at this point the various positions that are sometimes erroneously attributed to positivism:

1. Positivists do not necessarily deny the *importance* of morality. Positivists need not be moral sceptics of any sort. Indeed Bentham was centrally concerned with the moral criticism of law with a view to its reform.

2. Positivists do not deny that morality influences the content of law. Obviously, legislators often enact particular laws because of their moral convictions, and the law is influenced in its content by the moral views prevailing in society generally. But a rule does not *become* law (according to the positivists) until it has been laid down in a source such as a statute or a decided case.

3. Positivists do not deny that judges sometimes decide cases by reference to moral values, or considerations of social policy. What they *do* deny is that judges have to make moral judgments in working out what the existing law is. Having established what the relevant legal rules are, however, the judge may discover that these rules do not give an answer in the case he is dealing with. Since the pre-existing *law* does not give an answer, the judge must decide the case on the basis of extra-legal considerations. In doing so he will establish a new legal rule. But what makes the rule a legal rule is the fact that it has been laid down by a judge, not the fact that it was based on moral considerations.

4. Positivists do not deny that there may be a moral obligation to obey the law. They argue that the question of what the law is, and the question of whether it ought to be obeyed, are two separate questions. Indeed, positivists such as Bentham and Hart argue that our moral reflections on the scope of the obligation to obey the law are clarified by adopting a positivist conception of law.

79

Rules and the internal point of view

Positivists tend to see the legal order as a body of rules which have been "posited" or laid down by persons with law-making authority. This means that a positivist theory of law must offer an account of the nature of law-making authority. At the same time, positivists claim that the question of what the law *is* is separate from the question of whether we have an obligation to obey it. This means that their account of law-making authority must not be an account of moral legitimacy. Bentham objected to accounts of sovereignty and law-making authority that treated these notions as moral claims to obedience. The account of law-making authority offered by positivism must be quite independent of any theory about the basis of a moral obligation to obey the law. Similarly, positivists must offer accounts of what it is to have a "legal obligation" or a "legal right". Their accounts must clearly distinguish these concepts from the notion of moral obligation or a moral right.

Bentham and Austin approached these problems by treating statements about sovereignty, rights, and obligations, as straightforward statements of observable social fact. For example, a body of persons constituted the "sovereign" (the supreme law-making authority) in Austin's theory when that body was habitually obeyed by the bulk of the population, and did not itself habitually obey any other person or body; and a person was under a legal obligation to do a certain act when, in the event of non-compliance with a sovereign command, he was likely to suffer a sanction at the sovereign's behest. In each case a legal concept is treated as referring to observable social facts: "sovereignty" refers to regular patterns of obedience, and "obligation" refers to the likelihood of suffering a sanction.

Hart argues that this approach is inadequate. One cannot establish the separation of law and morals by simply reducing propositions of law to straightforward factual descriptions of regular patterns of behaviour. We can see this in relation to the concepts of "sovereignty", and "obligation".

Suppose that the sovereign, supreme law-maker in a certain legal system is an absolute monarch, Rex I. According to Austin, Rex I is the sovereign insofar as he is habitually obeyed by the bulk of the population. Now suppose that Rex I dies and is succeeded by his son, Rex II. Hart points out that we have, on Austin's theory, no reason for regarding Rex II as the new sovereign. Having only just "taken over", he has not yet issued any orders and has not yet been obeyed.

It follows that we cannot describe the bulk of the population as "habitually" obeying him. So, on Austin's definition of the sovereign, we cannot treat Rex II as the sovereign until he has issued some orders and been obeyed. What Austin lacks is the notion of a *rule* which *entitles* Rex II to succeed his father. His notion of a habit of obedience is a mere *regularity* of conduct, not a rule.

According to Austin, obligations exist insofar as the failure to obey the sovereign's orders is regularly followed by the application of sanctions. In stating that someone has a legal obligation we are saying that he is likely to suffer a sanction if he does not comply. But in Hart's view, this simply will not do as an analysis of the concept of obligation. The likelihood of suffering a sanction might *oblige* someone to act in a certain way, as I might be obliged to hand my money to a gunman who threatens me. But it would not impose an *obligation* on me. When we speak of someone as having a certain obligation, we are invoking a rule as a standard that ought to be complied with. When a judge refers to the defendant's obligations as a reason for ordering him to pay damages, the judge is invoking a rule as a *justification* for her decision, she is not predicting the likely application of a sanction.

By treating the legal order as a body of observable regularities of conduct, pure and simple, Austin was unable to accommodate such notions as right, entitlement, obligation, and justification. What Austin needed, according to Hart, in place of the notion of a regular pattern of conduct, was the concept of an accepted rule. How, then, does an accepted rule differ from a mere regularity?

Suppose that the great majority of people go to the cinema every Saturday night. This regular pattern of conduct does not demonstrate that they accept a rule that they *ought* to go to the cinema every Saturday. On the other hand, motorists regularly stop at red lights: here, there does seem to be an accepted rule that they ought to stop. So what is the difference?

Hart says that where an accepted rule exists, the regular pattern of conforming behaviour (which Hart calls "the external aspect") is accompanied by an "internal aspect". Where a rule exists people who do not conform to the regular pattern are criticised and the criticism is regarded as justified. The regular pattern of conduct is regarded as a standard that ought to be complied with. People regard the rule from an "internal point of view", treating it as a reason for action. This internal point of view carries along with it a certain vocabulary. People speak of what "ought" to be done; they treat the rule (in some cases) as imposing "obligations" or as

81

conferring "rights". The rule is treated, not as a simple observable regularity, but as an appropriate basis for the evaluation and criticism of conduct.

Hart uses these basic ideas to explain the nature of law-making authority, and to explicate the concepts of "legal obligation" and "legal right". The basis of law-making authority lies, not in habits of obedience as Austin would hold, but in the acceptance of a basic rule that entitles or authorises the enactment of new legal rules. These rules will be spoken of as imposing obligations and conferring rights, insofar as the rules are regarded from an internal point of view, as standards that ought to be complied with.

Powers and secondary rules

Bentham and Austin treated all laws as duty-imposing. In Bentham's case this approach was linked to his view that every law is a restriction on liberty. Being a restriction on liberty, every law is, in itself, an evil which needs to be justified by reference to its utilitarian value.

In Hart's opinion, this tendency to reduce all law to a single pattern ignores the differing social functions of different laws. Not all laws restrict conduct by imposing duties: some laws are intended to provide facilities, to make available options that would not otherwise exist. For example, the law that confers the power to make a will is not a restriction on conduct: it does not compel us to do anything, but merely offers us a means of controlling the disposition of our property on death if we wish to do so. Such power-conferring laws are, Hart argues, fundamentally different from duty-imposing laws.

Power-conferring laws confer the power to alter legal rights and legal relations, and to amend or enact legal rules. Examples of legal powers are the power to make a will, the power to make a binding contract, the power to enact by-laws, and so on. Rules which confer powers are an example of what Hart calls "secondary rules".

"Primary rules" are rules about conduct, of the kind we are all familiar with: do not kill, do not steal, always stop at a red light, etc. "Secondary rules" are rules about other rules: about how to alter other rules, how to interpret them, how to enact them, and how to recognize them as valid rules. The most important type of secondary rule, in Hart's theory, is the type he calls a "rule of recognition". The nature of such a rule is best explained in the following way.

Suppose that we all lived in a fairly simple society that lacked courts and legislatures, but where a number of straightforward primary rules were widely accepted. Everyone, or at least the great majority of people, accepted that you ought not to murder, or steal, or cheat, or tell lies. However firm the moral consensus was, such a society, possessing only primary rules, would face a number of serious problems. To begin with there would inevitably be arguments about exactly what the rules required in specific cases. For example, does the rule against murder extend to euthanasia? Or to abortion? Does the rule against "cheating" extend to non-disclosure of relevant facts in concluding an agreement? In a society without such a strong moral consensus, these disputes would extend beyond questions of how the rules are to be interpreted and would reach the issue of what rules should be observed in the first place (for instance, "What's wrong with stealing, if the existing distribution of property is unjust?"). Yet, even if people could not agree on what exactly the primary rules were, or on what set of rules would be just, they could probably agree on the necessity of having rules of some sort. So the answer would seem to be the acceptance of some basic "rule of recognition" which provides the criteria for identifying the primary rules to be regarded as binding.

A simple rule of recognition might specify that only the rules carved on certain stone tablets were to be treated as binding. But a rule of recognition of this kind would render the primary rules immune from change. So the rule of recognition is likely to specify some sources of authority who are empowered to alter and enact new primary rules.

According to Hart, every legal system contains a basic rule of recognition by reference to which we can identify the fundamental sources of law. For example, in the United Kingdom the most important sources of law are statutes and precedents: we can establish that these are sources of law by reference to the basic rule of recognition. But how do we discover what the content of the rule of recognition is? Hart's answer is that the rule of recognition is a rule accepted by officials. If we examine the behaviour of officials deciding disputes we will discover a regular pattern of conduct (the external aspect of the rule) that consists in always deciding disputes by reference to the rules emanating from certain sources (statutes and precedents, in the case of the United Kingdom). The officials regard this way of deciding cases as the *proper* way; they regard the rule of recognition as a standard that ought to be complied with (*i.e.* they take the internal point of view). These facts about official behaviour can be established by empirical observation. By reference to them, the content of the existing law can be determined.

This means that it is the existence of a basic rule of recognition that makes the legal order into a body of publicly ascertainable rules. In the absence of such a basic rule, we would have to regulate our conduct according to our own conceptions of justice and moral right. Where publicly ascertainable rules exist and are generally followed, our moral convictions may lead us to adopt *those* rules as a guide even where we consider them to be less than ideal.

It can now be seen how Hart's positivism (his claim that law is separate from morality) is directly linked to his idea of the rule of recognition. It is the whole point of the rule of recognition to provide a body of publicly ascertainable rules: the rules are publicly ascertainable in that their content can be established simply by reference to empirical facts, without making any moral judgments. Hence, the separation of law and morality is essential to law's basic function.

The legal system

According to Hart, a legal system can be said to exist when two conditions are satisfied:

1. Officials must accept and apply a basic rule of recognition. They must "accept" the rule in the sense that they regard it from an internal point of view, as a standard that ought to be complied with.
2. The population at large must generally comply with the primary rules.

But it is not a part of the meaning of the concept of "legal system" that the population should "accept" the primary rules or the rule of recognition: only the officials need take an internal point of view. This is not to deny that a legal system which did not rest on some degree of popular acceptance might be both morally objectionable and politically unstable: but these moral and political requirements are not semantic features of the concept of "legal system" itself.

Once we have passed from a society having only primary rules to a society having a basic rule of recognition, new concepts become applicable. In a simple society with only primary rules, rules "exist" only when they are accepted and observed in people's conduct. To invoke a rule against theft (for example) in such a context is to point to a regular pattern of conduct (the external aspect) as a standard which ought to be complied with (the internal point of view). But, when there is a rule of recognition, rules can be said to "exist" in another sense. Rules which emanate from the sources identified by the basic rule of recognition are "valid"; and a "valid" rule can exist even if it is not accepted or applied by anyone. Suppose that an Act of Parliament was passed in 1800 and has never been applied in a case since then. Indeed, the judges, lawyers, and police have completely forgotten of the Act's existence. Such an Act would not be accepted or applied by anyone; the rules that it contains would not be exemplified by anyone's conduct and would have no "external aspect": but the Act, if it has not been repealed, would still be a valid Act, and the rules that it contains would be valid rules.

In this way, Hart has provided a solution for the problem of the relationship between efficacy and legal validity. Legal validity is to be distinguished from efficacy, for a rule may be totally ineffective and yet be valid. But we should not be led to detach validity completely from considerations of efficacy. We feel that the laws of Tsarist Russia are now invalid because they are no longer effective. Hart's theory shows how an ineffective rule may still be valid provided that it emanates from the basic rule of recognition: but in order to be a valid rule, the legal system to which it belongs must, as a whole, be an effective legal system.

The central role that Hart gives to "officials" in his theory is both striking and curious. Hart nowhere tells us just what an "official" is or how we recognize one. Since we identify the *law* by reference to official behaviour (in the form of the rule of recognition) we cannot identify officials by reference to the law. Presumably Hart has it in mind that we should identify officials by some sociological criterion, but he does nothing to explain the nature of such a test.

What if someone described Hart's theory as simply saying "The law is whatever the officials say it is"? Would that be a fair summary of Hart's views? Well, we must begin by appreciating that the rule of recognition is not just a regular pattern of official behaviour. It is not just what the officials regularly *do*: it represents a standard that they believe they *ought* to comply with. Since it is a genuine *rule* that they accept, it is possible for the officials to misapply it. Suppose that the officials accept a rule requiring them to enforce Acts of Parliament. If an official one day fails to apply an Act (because, say, he disapproves of it) we can describe him as having got the law wrong, or as having failed to apply the law. Thus it is not true that, in Hart's theory, whatever an official does or says represents the law.

But, in another sense, officials do occupy a key position for Hart. Suppose that the House of Lords and all the other senior English judges, decided that they were not going to enforce Acts of Parliament anymore, but were going to enforce decrees of the Workers' Revolutionary Council. If they succeeded in doing this, and if the bulk of the population complied with the new decrees rather than with the old enactments of Parliament, the judges would have effected a change in the rule of recognition. From the point of view of the *old* rule of recognition, the judges' actions would be unlawful: but then, that old rule of recognition no longer exists. So in this way official behaviour does indeed provide the bedrock criterion of legitimacy for Hart.

On some points the existing rule of recognition may give uncertain guidance or no guidance at all. If, for example, we are considering the effect on parliamentary sovereignty of Britain joining the EEC, the established practice of the officials gives us little assistance in formulating an answer. Hart's view on these uncertainties in the basic rule of recognition seems to be that the questions with which they face us are not really legal questions at all. Though framed in legal terms and debated *as if* they were legal in nature, the questions are of a political or ideological nature; but, once a decision has been given by the judges, the decision *establishes* law on that point.

Several of Hart's critics have felt that law and legitimacy cannot be explicated by reference to a model that gives the central role to official behaviour. Thus Lon Fuller has criticised Hart for viewing law as a one-way projection of authority, from the officials down. Fuller emphasises that our notions of legality import a degree of reciprocity between rulers and ruled and he accuses Hart of completely neglecting this.

Judicial decisions

I said earlier that legal positivists do not deny that judges sometimes decide cases by reference to moral values or social policy considerations. It will be necessary for the judge to do this, according to the positivists, whenever the existing rules of law fail to give a determinate answer in the specific case. In claiming that law is separate from morality, the positivists are denying that moral judgments are necessary to discover what the existing law is: but discovering the existing law is not always enough in itself to decide a case. Where the law does not give an answer, the judge must establish, by his decision, a *new* legal rule, and this he will do on the basis of extra-legal considerations of morality and social policy.

This view of judicial decision-making seems to suggest that, when we are considering an innovative precedent, we should be able to distinguish between the rule that the court laid down in its decision and the (moral or social policy) arguments that led them to their decision. It is necessary for the positivist to make this distinction because he wishes to claim that, although the moral views of judges and legislators inevitably influence their decisions to introduce this or that new law, what *makes* a rule into law is the fact that it has been laid down in an authoritative source, and *not* the moral reasons that support it.

But is it possible to perform the analytical separation required by the positivist theory? Take, for example, the case of *Donoghue* v. *Stevenson* ([1932] A.C. 562). Was Lord Atkin's "neighbour principle" the "rule" laid down in that case? Or was it simply Lord Atkin's reason for laying down a much more specific rule concerning the liability of manufacturers? Indeed, we saw in the Introduction to this book that it is not at all clear that case law is a matter of "rules" at all. It is always open to a later judge to narrow the "rule" laid down in an earlier case, or to create a new exception to that rule. So in what sense is the latter judge bound by a rule established in the earlier case?

It was objections of this kind that led the American Realists to reject the whole notion of law as consisting of binding rules. Hart's response to the arguments of the Realists is, however, a depressingly irrelevant one. Hart distinguishes between formalists and rule-sceptics. Formalists look upon the law as a self-contained body of standards that determine, by deductive logic, the correct answer in every case. Hart regards this as a mistaken view. Language, he says, has an "open texture": each word has a range of clear cases that it definitely applies to, and a range of "penumbral" cases where it is not clear whether the word applies or not. Language does not pick out and classify situations with surgical precision. It follows that no set of rules can give pre-determined answers in every possible case, and formalism must therefore be wrong.

In Hart's view, rule-sceptics (American Realists) simply make the opposite mistake to the formalists. They treat rules and language as if they had no core of settled meaning and gave no determinate guidance at all. But the fact that concepts have a penumbra of indeterminacy does not mean that they are altogether devoid of

87

meaning. Words have a core of settled meaning, rules have a core of settled application: in some cases the judges must have recourse to moral and social policy considerations, but in the great majority of cases the judge simply has to apply an established legal rule.

But, combining what is said above with the discussion in the Introduction (pp. 2–9 above) of the "black letter" view of law, the student should now be able to see the inadequacy of Hart's reply. The objection to the view of law as a body of rules does not rest on an appeal to the indeterminacy of language. Rather, the appeal is to established practices of legal reasoning such as the practice of distinguishing, of narrowing earlier rulings, and of creating unenvisaged exceptions to rules. It is virtually impossible to explain such practices on a model of judicial decisions that treats them as simply "laying down" rules by which later courts are "bound".

The errors of rival theories

Any theory of law should be capable of explaining how rival theories have been led into error. If law really is separate from morality, why have some people thought otherwise? If law is just the rules enforced by officials, how have intelligent men been led to confuse it with justice and moral right? Part of the answer might be thought to be the shared vocabulary of law (legal rights and moral rights, legal duties and moral duties, etc.) but this is scarcely a sufficient explanation on its own, for it does not tell us how it is that law and morality have come to share so many of the same concepts.

Hart goes some way in exploring the features of law that link it closely to morality. These are, principally, (1) the connection between rules and the principle of formal justice, and (2) the shared content of legal systems. We shall examine each of these in turn.

Rules and formal justice

Hart adopts a well-known distinction between "formal" and "substantive" justice. The principle of formal justice is that like cases should be treated alike, and different cases should be treated differently. Different conceptions of justice offer different explanations of what counts as a "like" or "unlike" case. If I believe in distribution according to need, and you believe in distribution according to desert, we hold different substantive conceptions of justice. But we are agreed on the principle of *formal* justice: our

88

disagreement is a disagreement about what should count as a material difference to justify differential treatment. Is *need* relevant, or only *desert*?

The two aspects of justice (formal and substantive) reflect two different problems of justice in the law. On the one hand, the law may be criticised as substantively unjust. An egalitarian may disapprove of laws based on a Nozickean theory of justice; a Nozickean would disapprove of the law of a Rawlsian community. But on the other hand, whether we approve or disapprove of the substantive conception of justice on which the law is based, we may scrutinise the legal system from the point of view of formal justice. Justice in its formal dimension is essentially a matter of the consistent application of rules. Formal justice requires that, given the criteria of likeness and difference which are established in the law, these criteria should indeed be the determining element in judicial and official decisions applying the law.

Since Hart treats law as a body of rules, it is easy for him to fit the value of formal justice into his theory. If judicial decisions are concerned with the application of rules, the value of formal justice will have an immediate relevance to the moral scrutiny of such decisions. This, in Hart's view, is enough to explain the close connections often thought to exist between the concepts of law and justice. What Hart does not seem to perceive is the way in which conceptions of formal justice could be developed much more extensively in ways that would erode legal positivism quite fundamentally. For example, if the consistent application of rules is a requirement of *justice*, then litigants presumably have a moral right that the rules should be applied consistently. Is it not possible that *that moral right* is just what their legal rights amount to? In other words, could one not argue that legal rights are really a variety of moral rights, based on the value of formal justice? And if formal justice is a matter of consistency, could not that requirement of consistency extend beyond the application of posited black letter rules? Might it not require that judges, in introducing *new* legal rules, should do so only by reference to the concepts and criteria implicit in the existing law? And would this not suggest that the account of legal reasoning as the application of pre-existing rules interspersed with moral or policy decisions is itself inadequate? In examining the legal theory of Ronald Dworkin, in the next chapter, we will be turning to a line of thought that develops these suggestions into a basic rejection of legal positivism.

The shared content of legal systems

At the start of this chapter I described legal positivists as making two main claims: (1) that we can identify the existing law without making any moral judgments, and (2) that in speaking of laws as conferring rights and imposing duties, we are not making any kind of moral judgment.

Both of these claims are essentially about the language and criteria characteristic of the internal point of view. It is judges, lawyers and citizens—*i.e.* participants in the legal system—who invoke the rule of recognition as a criterion, and who speak of laws as conferring rights. The question about the separation of law and morality is primarily a question about the participants' point of view. But there are other aspects to the problem, and these other aspects arise from a more *external*, theoretical point of view.

Suppose that the Mafia gained complete control of the United Kingdom, they overthrew the established government, demolished the apparatus of courts, police forces, and so on. In the place of these institutions they issued their own decrees, which they enforced by their own officials. Would this count as a "legal system"?

One traditional answer says that it would not. It is essential to the concept of a legal system (it can be argued) that the apparatus of rules, courts and government, is aimed at the common good; or is intended to implement some conception of justice. A regime intended only to exploit the civil population cannot be properly described as a legal system no matter how many of the institutional arrangements of rules and officials it deploys.

To the legal positivist, such a response is likely to seem an unnecessary confusion of law and morality. The concepts of law and legal system, the positivist will argue, should be explicated in terms of purely factual, non-moral criteria. Legal systems can be put to good purposes or to bad: the enforcement of justice, or the extermination of Jews. Our account of what a legal system *is* must therefore be formulated in morally neutral terms that make no reference to the good or bad *purposes* of the system. Thus, for Hart, a legal system is characterised by the existence of a rule of recognition and a body of primary rules which are, for whatever reason, generally complied with. Given those formal features, it is logically possible for a legal system to have *any* content, just or unjust.

Nevertheless, there is a high degree of convergence in the rules that legal systems contain. They all contain rules prohibiting violence and theft, defining and regulating property and agreements, and governing relationships within the family. This convergence of content is not, in Hart's view, a coincidence. It does not just "happen to be the case" that legal systems have these rules. If, says Hart, we assume that legal systems consist of rules which will make human survival possible, the basic facts of human nature and human circumstances make rules of the kind outlined a necessity. Thus, the typical content that we associate with legal systems is not just a contingent fact about those systems; but nor is it a logical feature of the concept of "legal system" (legal systems do not, as a matter of *logical* necessity, have to serve the common good in any sense). The shared content of legal systems is a natural necessity. It is a necessary feature of legal systems, given certain basic facts of human nature and circumstances.

Legal obligation and the internal point of view

On one view, the law can be spoken of as conferring rights and imposing obligations only insofar as we regard it as morally binding. A law that is not morally binding cannot, it is argued, impose any obligation on us. Since lawyers talk about the law in the language of rights and duties (rather than, say, the language of force and coercion) they are committed to a view of the law as morally binding.

Hart wants to resist this line of argument and to claim that legal discourse does not assume any particular moral attitude towards the law. Judgments about the existence of legal rights and obligations leave the moral question of what ought to be done quite open. Yet Hart does not want to reduce legal discourse to some form of simple fact-stating discourse. Propositions about the existence of legal obligations, for example, are not simple predictions of the application of sanctions, or the likely reactions of courts. Judges invoke the parties' legal obligations as reasons for action; the language of law (rights, duties, ought, etc.) is essentially concerned to *prescribe* conduct, not to *describe* it. The problem for Hart is clear. How can a legal positivist resist the conclusion that propositions of law are a type of moral judgment without reducing them to predictive or fact-stating propositions? How can one separate law from morality unless one approaches law from a purely external point of view? How can Hart remain a legal positivist while claiming that the characteristic concepts of legal discourse derive their meaning from an "internal point of view": a point of view that regards the law as a body of standards that ought to be complied with?

One approach is offered by the legal theory of Hans Kelsen. Kelsen, like Hart, emphasised the contrast between reductive approaches to the legal order that treat it as an apparatus of systematic coercion, and the lawyer's distinctive point of view, that regards the legal order as a body of "valid" norms. To reflect the lawyer's point of view, and to make sense of his language, it was necessary, in Kelsen's opinion, to adopt the basic presupposition that the authorities in effective control ought to be obeyed. But this basic presupposition (or basic norm, as Kelsen called it) did not commit one to moral approval of the law, for the presupposition could be made for the strictly limited purpose of reproducing the content of the legal order as a body of valid norms.

Hart rejects Kelsen's assumption that "valid" means "ought to be obeyed". According to Hart, the judgment that a rule is valid is not a judgment that it ought to be obeyed, but a judgment that the rule emanates from the rule of recognition. This argument leads Hart to reject Kelsen's theory of the basic norm, for the following reasons. When Kelsen is confronted with an ultimate constitution or rule of recognition he asks, in effect, "what makes this rule valid?" Hart sees the basic norm as Kelsen's answer to that question. But Hart rejects the question itself as meaningless. The rule of recognition is itself the ultimate criterion of legal validity. To say that a rule is valid simply means that it emanates from the rule of recognition. Accordingly it makes no sense to ask whether the rule of recognition is itself "valid", any more than it would make sense to ask whether the metre-bar in Paris is *really* a metre long.

Hart misses the point of Kelsen's theory, which is essentially to comprehend, within the context of a positivist theory, the "internal point of view". Hart himself says that concepts such as right, duty, ought, and validity are characteristic of the internal point of view, and that is a point of view which regards the law as a body of standards that ought to be complied with. Does it not follow that propositions about legal rights, duties, validity, and so on, express conclusions about what ought to be done? But how can this be if law is separate from morality?

Much depends here on what we mean by the separation of law and morality. Suppose that we accept two claims:

1. The law is never morally conclusive. Even given that the law requires that I act in a certain way, it remains an open

question whether morally I ought to act in that way. The existence of the law may *affect* the morality of the action, but it does not conclusively determine it.

2. The mere fact that a rule is a just and good rule does not make it a law. To be a law, it must emanate from an authorised source. Equally, the fact that a rule is unjust does not show that it *is not* a law, if the rule does in fact emanate from an authorised source.

These two claims are close to the heart of legal positivism, and explain much of that theory's plausibility. But they are in fact *consistent* with the claim that propositions of law are a type of moral judgment.

If we reflect on Hart's account of the need for a rule of recognition to provide the certainty that is lacking in a society with primary rules alone, we will see that the positivist view of law as publicly ascertainable rules reflects an important moral dimension of the law. If we accept the need for publicly ascertainable rules, and we accept that legal rules are publicly ascertainable, we must also accept that the whole point of having laws will be defeated if people are willing to comply with the law only when they consider it to be just. We can view the law as binding us morally even when we disapprove of its content. Thus, the claim that legal obligation is a type of moral obligation is quite consistent with the positivist idea that law is law, be it just or unjust. Since the basis of the moral obligation lies in law's publicly ascertainable nature, the claim is also consistent with the idea that laws must emanate from authoritative sources, and that being "just" is not enough to make a rule into a law. Since any moral obligation may be overridden by conflicting obligations, the claim that legal obligation is a type of moral obligation is also consistent with the idea that the law is never completely conclusive of what we morally ought to do: there may be circumstances when it is our moral duty to break the law.

The starting point for our discussion was the contrast between the reductive external view of the legal order as a system of power, sanctions and threats, and the internal view (of the lawyer, the judge, and most citizens) of the law as imposing obligations, conferring rights, and so on. The conclusion we are led to is that the internal point of view can only be understood as a particular moral attitude towards the law: not necessarily moral approval of the law's content, but moral acceptance of the general obligation to comply with publicly ascertainable legal rules. Propositions of law are, on this view, a variety of moral judgment. They represent a judgment from the point of view of a specific range of considerations: considerations relating to the need for order and for compliance with rules of which we may disapprove.

The ambiguity of legal positivism

The last section should have alerted the reader to the fact that the claims of legal positivism are far from clear. For I was concerned to argue, in that section, that legal positivism itself rests on a particular moral perspective. Positivists wish to portray the law as a body of rules that can be ascertained in some more or less uncontroversial way, quite independently of our differing moral judgments. But (I was arguing) this approach itself rests on an understanding of the distinctive moral significance of law. It is precisely the *public* nature of law that gives it its moral claim on our conduct. It is the separation of law and morality at one level that provides the moral foundations of law at another.

On the view of legal positivism that I have been describing so far, every legal system must have a basic rule of recognition that identifies the laws of that system by publicly ascertainable characteristics (having been laid down in a statute, etc.). A rule of recognition might, to a limited extent, impart some criteria of a more ethical and less ascertainable nature, but the general public character of law must be preserved. A "rule of recognition" that simply said "all those rules which are just are legal rules" would not provide the basis for a legal system. It would simply throw us back on our individual views of justice and would not represent a significant improvement on the situation of having only primary rules.

There is however a rival interpretation of legal positivism according to which positivism makes much more modest claims. On this view the positivist simply claims that it is not a necessary truth that law and morality must coincide. Laws may or may not be publicly ascertainable. Rules of recognition may or may not throw us back on our individual moral judgment. Legal positivism need not, on this view, take any stance on such issues. All that positivism *does* claim is that it is conceivable that one might have a legal system with unjust rules: such a notion is not self-contradictory. Legal positivism of this kind, however, is so lacking in content that it can scarcely be regarded as a theory of law at all. We will return to the problems that it poses in the following chapter.

SELECTED READING

H. L. A. HART, *The Concept of Law* (1961).

H. L. A. HART, *Essays in Jurisprudence and Philosophy* (1983), Essays 1 and 2.

NEIL MACCORMICK, *H. L. A. Hart* (1981).

ROLF SARTORIUS, "Hart's Concept of Law" in R. SUMMERS (Ed.) *More Essays in Legal Philosophy* (1971).

R. A. DUFF, "Legal Obligation and the Moral Nature of Law" (1980) *Juridical Review*, p. 61.

N. E. SIMMONDS, "The Nature of Propositions of Law" (1984) *Rechtstheorie* 96.

6. Dworkin

If H. L. A. Hart may be regarded as the foremost exponent of legal positivism in this century, there can be no doubt that Ronald Dworkin ranks as his principal opponent. As we shall see, Dworkin attacks the whole idea that there is some fundamental test or criterion in the nature of a rule of recognition that serves to distinguish law from morality. Dworkin offers a powerful and stimulating analysis of the nature of legal reasoning, and has posed new questions for legal theory. If, at the end of the day, the achievements of his critique of positivism remain uncertain, that is perhaps as much the fault of ambiguities in the positivist position itself, as of difficulties in Dworkin's own argument.

Rules and principles

Hart claims that we can work out what the existing law is by reference to the basic rule of recognition. The rule of recognition identifies certain sources (statutes, judicial decisions) as sources of law: a rule counts as "law" if it emanates from such a source. Sometimes it will not be clear whether or not a rule applies to a given case. This is because of the "open texture" of language. For example, it may be unclear whether a rule relating to "vehicles" should be applied to a milk-float, a pedal car, or a pair of roller skates, since it is not clear whether these count as "vehicles". In such cases, the court has to exercise its discretion, and will have regard to policy considerations (including the presumed policy objectives of the rule) and to considerations of fairness. But in the majority of cases, no such exercise of discretion is necessary: a motor car, for example, is clearly a "vehicle" and the rule must be applied.

Dworkin challenges this general picture of law and legal reasoning. He begins by discussing a United States case, *Riggs* v. *Palmer*, although he tells us that almost any case in a law school casebook would serve his purpose as well. In *Riggs* v. *Palmer* a murderer claimed that he was entitled to inherit under the will of his victim. The will was valid, and was in the murderer's favour. The existing rules of testamentary succession contained no exceptions relating to such a case. The court decided, however, that the application of the rules was subject to general principles of law, including the principle that no man should profit from his own wrong. They held that the murderer was not entitled to the inheritance.

Riggs v. *Palmer* shows us, according to Dworkin, that the law does not consist entirely of rules: it also includes *principles*. Principles differ from rules in a number of related ways:

1. Rules apply in an "all or nothing" fashion. If a rule applies, and it is a valid rule, the case must be decided in accordance with it. A principle, on the other hand, gives a *reason* for deciding the case one way, but not a *conclusive reason*. A principle may be a binding legal principle, and may apply to a case, and yet the case need not necessarily be decided in accordance with the principle. This is because principles *conflict* and must be *weighed* against each other: see 2 and 3 below.

2. Valid rules cannot conflict. If two rules appear to conflict, they cannot both be treated as valid. Legal systems have doctrinal techniques for resolving such apparent conflicts of valid rules, *e.g.* the maxim *lex posterior derogat priori*. Legal principles, on the other hand, can conflict and still be binding legal principles.

3. Because they can conflict, legal principles have a dimension of *weight* which rules do not have. Rules are either valid or not valid: there is no question of one rule "outweighing" another. But principles must be balanced against each other.

This analysis may at first seem hard to square with Dworkin's own discussion of *Riggs* v. *Palmer*. For was that not a case where a principle came into conflict with a rule (the statutes regulating testamentary succession)? And does not Dworkin's analysis suggest that principles conflict only with other principles, and not with rules? The answer is that *Riggs* v. *Palmer* is in fact, despite appearances, a clash between principles, not between rules and principles. The rules of testamentary succession were binding on the court by virtue of certain underpinning principles, such as the principle that "the enactments of a democratic legislature should be enforced according to their clear wording". This principle (or one like it) came into conflict with the principle that "no man shall profit from his own wrong". The court, in deciding that the latter principle was decisive, was not deciding that that principle would *always* outweigh the principle about enforcing statutes. Rather, they were deciding that the effect of allowing a murderer to inherit from his victim would be such a serious infringement of the values protected by the "no profit" principle, that that principle should prevail *in those circumstances.*

This analysis enables us to see how the courts can *change* the law while *applying* the law. At first this seems paradoxical: one might argue that if the courts change the law they must do so by deviating from the strict application of the law. However, we can see from the example of *Riggs* v. *Palmer* that a court may create a new exception to the established rules, but do so on the basis of legal principles. Thus *Riggs* v. *Palmer* created a new exception to the general rules on testamentary succession ("a murderer may not inherit under the will of his victim") but justified that exception by a legal principle ("no man shall profit from his own wrong").

Principles and positivism

Suppose that we accept Dworkin's analysis of *Riggs* v. *Palmer*, what does all this have to do with legal positivism? It is not enough merely to point out that Hart does not mention legal principles, for that does not show that they are in any way inconsistent with his theory. Why shouldn't we treat Dworkin as simply making a useful addition to Hart's theory?

One problem is that *Riggs* v. *Palmer* would not even qualify as a hard case in Hart's theory. According to Hart, hard cases where the law is uncertain are the result of the "open texture" of language. We are uncertain about the law because these cases do not fall clearly within or without the wording of the relevant rules. But this is scarcely an adequate account of *Riggs* v. *Palmer*. That case was not concerned with any uncertainty about the exact range of applicability of the concepts "valid will", "profit", "wrong" or anything else.

Nevertheless, we may feel that Hart could meet this point by allowing that in some cases legal standards conflict with each other, and that this produces a type of uncertainty in the law not explicable by reference to the "open texture" of language. There seems nothing inconsistent with legal positivism *here*.

The importance of Dworkin's analysis as an attack on positivism can be appreciated only when we come to Dworkin's account of how legal principles are identified. He claims that legal principles cannot be identified by anything resembling Hart's rule of recognition. A principle may be already a legal principle although no court has ever formulated it or laid it down as a principle. For example, suppose that no lawyer or judge has ever mentioned the principle that no man shall profit from his own wrong. It might still be possible to demonstrate that that principle is an existing legal principle if one could show that the principle provides an appropriate justification for a range of established black letter rules and decisions (*e.g.* a gambler cannot sue for his winnings, a prostitute cannot sue for her earnings, a person injured in an illegal enterprise cannot claim compensation, a party cannot rely on a mistake induced by his own fraud in order to avoid or enforce a contract). Thus we cannot identify principles simply by consulting certain sources, but only by engaging in a moral or political discussion of what principles should be invoked to justify the black letter rules of law.

Two strategies for reconciling principles with positivism may be contrasted. On the one hand, the positivist may argue that principles are indeed a part of the law, but that they can be identified by some version of the rule of recognition. On the other hand, the positivist may concede that principles cannot be identified by a basic rule of recognition, but may argue that this is because they are not in reality a part of the law: they are extra-legal, moral considerations that are applied by the courts, in the exercise of their discretion, when the legal rules fail to give a clear and determinate answer. We shall examine each of these two responses in turn.

The rule of recognition and the soundest theory

Dworkin does not argue that all moral principles are *ipso facto* legal principles. Some principles are legal principles and others are not. We might therefore attempt to argue along the following lines: "Dworkin accepts a distinction between legal and non-legal principles. He therefore must hold that there is some criterion that distinguishes legal from non-legal principles. But the idea that, in each legal system, there is some such basic criterion is the essential core of Hart's theory of the rule of recognition. Dworkin's theory therefore *itself* depends upon some notion of a basic rule of recognition."

Dworkin's response is to claim that Hart's theory of the rule of recognition does not simply claim that there is a criterion distinguishing law from non-law. Hart must claim, according to Dworkin, that laws are identified by *pedigree* not by *content, i.e.* a rule counts as a law not because it is just or fair (a matter of its *content*) but because it has been laid down or established in a statute or a case (a matter of *source* or *pedigree*). The whole point of having a rule of recognition, according to Hart, is to provide a body of rules which will be publicly ascertainable, in the sense that we can work out what the rules are without falling back on our judgments about justice or moral right. According to Dworkin, Hart's general thesis only makes sense if the rule of recognition identifies the law by criteria of pedigree. If the rule said something like "all those rules which are just are legal rules" it would provide no greater certainty than do our differing views of justice.

Legal principles are not identified by their pedigree. It is not necessary that a principle should have been laid down in a statute or a case. The judge who first formulates a legal principle formulates it as an existing part of the law and not as a legislative innovation of his own. In general, principles are identified by showing that they are embedded in the established rules and decisions, in the sense that the principle provides a suitable justification for the black letter rules.

Dworkin describes a hypothetical judge, called Hercules. Since he possesses superhuman powers, Hercules is able to carry out his judicial function in a far more thorough-going and articulate manner than could any actual judge. Nevertheless, the procedures and methods of argument employed by Hercules represent the form of decision-making that is presupposed by the methods of more fallible judges. Hercules does fully and explicitly what normal judges do in a more piecemeal and less self-conscious manner.

When Hercules decides a hard case (that is, a case that cannot be straightforwardly resolved on the basis of determinate black letter rules) he must begin by constructing a theory of law applicable to his jurisdiction. This theory of law will consist of an elaborate moral and political justification of the legal rules and institutions of the jurisdiction. For example, Hercules's jurisdiction may contain settled rules about legislative supremacy, and about the binding force of precedent. Hercules will need to work out a body of principles that will justify these rules. He must ask "What moral principles would serve to justify the doctrine of legislative supremacy? What moral principles underlie the doctrine of precedent?" Hercules must also consider the moral and political theory that seems to be at the basis of the substantive law of contract, tort, property, criminal law, welfare law, and so on. If Hercules carries out this task properly, the result will be a complex and integrated body of principles.

Now the criterion that, according to Dworkin, distinguishes legal from non-legal principles is this: a principle is a legal principle if it forms a part of the soundest theory of law that could be offered as a justification for the established legal rules and institutions. Constructing such a theory is, inevitably, a highly controversial matter involving complex and intractable issues of moral and political theory. It differs fundamentally from the process of identifying laws by reference to their sources that is envisaged by Hart's account of the rule of recognition.

There is a further respect in which Dworkin's theory differs from Hart's notion of the rule of recognition. In Hart's theory, we identify the law by reference to the basic rule of recognition; but we identify the basic rule of recognition by reference to the empirical facts of official behaviour: in this way, the content of the law can be established by a purely empirical inquiry, without asking any controversial moral questions. But this assumes that a judge, called upon to apply the rule of recognition, will apply the rule that is accepted by his fellow judges. This is fundamentally different from the position of Hercules. Hercules does not seek to apply the theory of law that is accepted by his judges: he seeks to apply the *soundest* theory of law, whether or not that theory is accepted by the other judges. Hercules must decide for himself which body of principles provides the best justification for the established laws. He is faced by a controversial question of political theory, not an empirical question about the behaviour of his colleagues on the bench.

Dworkin's idea of the "soundest theory of law" raises many problems. But for the time being, we can see the general way in which he responds to the claim that principles can in fact be identified by a basic rule of recognition. We may therefore pass to the alternative strategy for positivism, which focuses on the concept of "discretion".

Discretion and rights

The legal positivist does not deny that judges sometimes decide cases by reference to moral values. What the positivist *does* claim is that moral values need not be applied in determining what the existing law is: this can be determined by reference to the sources of rules identified by the rule of recognition. Sometimes, however, the established legal rules do not give a clear answer in a specific case. In such circumstances the judge must establish a *new* legal rule, and he will do so by reference to moral or social policy considerations. Since the law does not give an answer, he must step outside the law.

The positivist can apply this model to Dworkin's account of principles. He can claim that Dworkin's "principles" are simply moral considerations that the judge may have recourse to, in the exercise of his discretion, when the law does not give a clear answer. The positivist can then argue that the fact (if it is a fact) that principles cannot be identified by any basic rule of recognition does not refute legal positivism in general or Hart's theory in particular. To produce a refutation of positivism, Dworkin must offer compelling reasons for treating principles as a part of the existing law.

Dworkin does endeavour to produce such reasons. But before we turn to his arguments, let us note one initial difficulty for the positivist. If we treat principles as a part of the law, we can see why *Riggs* v. *Palmer* was a hard case, not because of any vagueness or "open texture" in the relevant rules, but because it involved a conflict between different legal standards: the principles requiring the enforcement of statutes according to their clear wording conflicted with the principle that no man should profit from his own wrong. But if principles are *not* part of the law, *Riggs* v. *Palmer* did not involve any conflict of legal standards. Nor did it involve any vagueness, uncertainty, or "open texture": the rules were clear and unambiguous. So why was it a hard case? If the law consists only of rules, *Riggs* v. *Palmer* was a case where the legal rules conflicted with desirable social policies or moral values. If the positivist takes *that* view of the case, he must hold one of two things. On the one hand, he may hold that *Riggs* v. *Palmer* was wrongly decided. On the other hand, he may hold that judges may refuse to apply the legal rules where they conflict with desirable social policies or moral values. But, if a judge can refuse to apply a rule whenever that seems best on the whole, he cannot be said to be *bound* by the rule.

The upshot of this argument is that, if we refuse to regard principles as a part of the law, we will be forced into one of two conclusions, each of which should be unacceptable to the legal positivist. On the one hand we will have to say that *Riggs* v. *Palmer* was not a *hard* case at all, but a case where the law was clear and the court simply failed to apply it. But, even if you feel that *Riggs* v. *Palmer was* wrongly decided, any competent lawyer should be able to spot this as a "hard" problematic case: the positivist view we are presently considering is unable to explain *why* the case was problematic. On the other hand, we could conclude that judges may set aside the established law whenever they think it best on the whole to do so. But if *that* is so, judges are never bound by rules at all, rules are of no real importance, and our "legal positivism" collapses into a version of rule-scepticism or "legal realism".

Dworkin offers an argument closely related to the above when he points out that courts in most jurisdictions now have the power to depart from their own earlier decisions. If principles are part of the law, we may regard the court's decision to depart from earlier precedents as itself regulated by legal principles. On this view, a court may alter the established rules only in the implementation of legal principles: even in altering the legal rules, the judge is applying the law. But if we hold that principles are *not* a part of the law, we must say that judges may depart from earlier decisions when, in the exercise of their discretion, they think it best to do so. If, however, judges can alter established rules in this way whenever they think it best (on moral or social policy grounds), they cannot be said to be bound by the rules at all. Thus, Dworkin argues, if principles are not part of the law, rules are not binding. Once again we are led to the conclusion that a rejection of the idea of legal principles leads, not to the positivist view of law as black letter rules, but to a thoroughgoing "rule scepticism".

The view that principles are not a part of the law, but are extralegal considerations applied in the exercise of discretion, is incompatible (according to Dworkin) not only with the idea of binding rules, but also with the idea that courts enforce the parties' rights. We regard courts, not as deciding to benefit the plaintiff at the defendant's expense (or vice versa), but as enforcing the plaintiff's or the defendant's rights. But if principles are not part of the law, it follows that courts in hard cases (which would certainly include the majority of cases reaching an appellate level) are exercising discretion; and if the court has a discretion about how it will decide the case, the parties cannot have a right to any particular decision.

Suppose that I am the trustee of £1,000 under a discretionary trust, and that you are one of six beneficiaries. If I have a discretion about how the money is distributed, it cannot be the case that you have a *right* to the whole £1,000. If you have a right to the whole sum, I cannot have a discretion about how it is distributed. Similarly, if a court has discretion about how it decides a case, neither the plaintiff nor the defendant can have a *right* to a decision in his favour. If courts in hard cases are exercising discretion, they cannot be enforcing pre-existing rights. But we ordinarily do think of courts as enforcing rights, and that is presupposed by the characteristic form of legal arguments. So we can refuse to admit principles as part of the law only by radically revising the way that we think and speak about law.

Some positivists are happy to accept this conclusion. They argue that people really only have established legal rights in clear cases. In hard cases, a court is not enforcing rights but exercising discretion on moral or social policy grounds. Lawyers and judges certainly talk *as if* they were concerned with the enforcement of pre-existing rights, but (it is argued) this form of speech is purely rhetorical and traditional, devoid of any real significance.

Principles and policies

Dworkin holds that courts should decide hard cases on grounds of principle, not policy. He intends this both as a *prescriptive* thesis, about what courts ought to do, and as a *descriptive* thesis, about what courts actually, for the most part, do.

Principles differ from policies in the following way. A principle defines and protects an individual right, whereas a policy stipulates a collective goal. Goals are those preferred states of affairs which the community seeks to pursue: *e.g.* a clean environment, a favourable balance of trade, an efficient transport system. Rights are individual claims which operate as "trumps" over collective goals. When we say that someone has, for example, a right of free speech, we mean (according to Dworkin) that that person's freedom of speech ought not to be interfered with even if that interference would serve collective goals, or the overall welfare of the community. Rights serve to protect the individual in that they work out certain individual interests which must not be interfered with merely to achieve some incremental increase in the general welfare. This is not to say that rights are absolute: rights (like the principles that define them) have a dimension of *weight*, and this weight is a matter of how far they will operate as trumps over policy considerations. Thus, although the right to free speech should not be abrogated merely in order to increase industrial productivity (for example), it might be the case that free speech could justifiably be suppressed for genuinely urgent reasons of national security. But, if a right truly *is* a right, it must have some weight to "trump" policy considerations: a right is not simply a desirable objective to be taken account of and traded off against other desirable objectives.

In many cases, we might think of a law as justified by either policy considerations or considerations of principle. Take, for example, laws against racial discrimination. These might be thought of as serving a policy of increasing racial harmony, by eliminating visible and institutionalised prejudice, and of increasing economic equality, by removing some of the obstacles that keep blacks in an economically disadvantaged position. But the laws might *also* be thought of as based on the principle that every man has a right not to be discriminated against on racial grounds. If the laws are justified solely on policy grounds, they can be justified only by showing that (a) they are more or less successful in attaining their objectives of racial harmony and increased economic equality, and (b) no other social goals of greater importance are damaged by the race laws. But, if the justification for these laws is a matter of *principle*, then their effects on racial harmony, economic equality, and rival social goals all cease to be decisive: people simply have (on this view) a *right* not to be discriminated against on racial grounds. Many critics doubt whether Dworkin has succeeded in establishing a distinction between principles and policies. They argue, for example, that we can only determine what rights people have by reference to some understanding of what will best serve the overall welfare, or collective goals. These issues are complex and cannot be adequately discussed here (though the discussion of rights in Part III of this book should help to cast some light on the problem). However, the following point should be noted. Dworkin makes the controversial claim that legal positivism and utilitarianism are connected not just historically, but conceptually: they are really two sides of the same theory. Dworkin's insistence on the distinction between principles and policies is really a part of his general rejection of classical utilitarianism: hence his insistence that rights operate as "trumps" over collective goals and over the general welfare. It is a mistake to imagine that the principle/policy distinction can be discussed in isolation from these deeper questions about utilitarianism, questions to which we can return in Part III. For the present, we must consider the argument that Dworkin offers in support of his claim that judges are, and ought to be, restricted to arguments of principle. These are the arguments from consistency, democracy and retroactivity.

1. *Consistency*

We expect the decisions of judges to be consistent; we expect like cases to be decided alike and different cases differently. But, Dworkin argues, such expectations are explicable only on the assumption that courts should base their decisions on grounds of principle. If judicial decisions were characteristically based on considerations of policy, there would be no reason to insist on the requirement that like cases be treated alike.

Many people find this argument a puzzling one. After all, it can be argued that the principle that like cases should be treated alike is a basic requirement of *rationality* applicable to all decisions of every kind. Why should Dworkin hold (as he may appear to) that it applies only to decisions based on principle?

To appreciate Dworkin's point one must realise that it rests on his basic idea of rights as trumps over collective goals. A community may have various goals (such as full employment, low inflation, a clean environment, high industrial productivity, longer holidays etc) and these goals will be to some extent incompatible: it will be necessary to trade off one goal against another. Having reached a certain level of industrial productivity, for example, we may decide that further increases should not be encouraged when they would be achieved at the cost of damage to the environment. But individual rights cannot be "traded off" in this way. If people have a right of free speech, they should be allowed to speak freely even if this harms the overall welfare: we cannot say that, at a certain point, we have achieved enough free speech and can begin restricting it (though, there will of course be limits in principle to *the right of free speech*). Thus rights commit us to future courses of action in a way that policies do not, since the policy is always subject to a general calculus of social goals.

2. *Democracy*

How is the role of the judiciary to be justified in a democratic society? How can non-elected judges justifiably make and shape the law? Should not law-making be left to the democratically elected legislature?

Dworkin believes that questions of this kind are bound to seem highly intractable so long as we think of judges in hard cases as establishing new rules on grounds of social policy. But the questions can receive an acceptable answer once we have realised that judges do not characteristically base their decisions on policy, but on principle.

Questions of policy concern the collective goals that we wish to pursue: new roads or new hospitals? High productivity or clean air? Such questions can plausibly be thought to depend on what people's *preferences* are. The democratic process is itself a mechanism for the expression of preferences, and legislatures are exposed to the expression of preferences more generally. It is therefore appropriate that questions of policy should be decided democratically, and should not be decided by judges.

With questions of principle it is otherwise. Principles define rights, and rights operate as trumps over collective goals. Rights are therefore (in a sense) rights *against* the majority. It is therefore appropriate for questions of principle to be decided not by democratically elected legislators, but by judges.

3. *Retroactivity*

Dworkin argues that when a court decides a case on grounds of principles it is enforcing a pre-existing right. When a court decides a case on grounds of policy, it is seeking to advance the attainment of some goal. If a court refuses to award me compensation because it believes that this will advance a desirable social policy, my rights are retrospectively being altered so as to serve collective goals.

It will be seen that this argument assumes that there *are* pre-existing rights in hard cases. But some positivists would deny this, holding that it only makes sense to speak of the court enforcing pre-existing rights when the law is clear. Of course, we disapprove of retrospective decision-making in any case, whether or not it abrogates established rights; but this may be because the parties are affected by a decision that was unforeseeable, and of which they had no reasonable notice. It is doubtful if decisions based on policy are any less foreseeable than decisions based on principle, given that Dworkin concedes the inherently controversial nature of both types of decision.

In constructing his "soundest theory of law" the judge will not be able to produce mutually consistent justifications for every single rule and decision. Whatever theory he constructs will have to treat some rules as "mistakes". This means that they are out of line with the general principles underlying the other rules and decisions of the jurisdiction. It does not mean that they cease to be binding rules:

they continue to have what Dworkin calls "enactment force", and they must be applied to those cases that fall within their expressed scope. But such rules lack "gravitational force", in that they cannot be used as the basis for an argument of principle which goes beyond the limited formula of the posited rule.

Exactly the same is true, according to Dworkin, of judicial precedents which were based on grounds of policy. These too have "enactment force", in that they establish a binding black letter rule, but they lack "gravitational force" in that they cannot be used as the basis for an argument of general principle.

The claims of legal positivism

Dworkin's account of law and legal reasoning differs fundamentally from the account offered by Hart. But is Dworkin's theory really inconsistent with legal positivism? We will discover that this question serves to reveal ambiguities in the central claims of legal positivism.

Suppose that Dworkin's judge Hercules is faced with a hard case on contract. Hercules will have to decide the case by reference to the "soundest theory of law" that he can construct. Such a theory will have to include a theory of contract: *i.e.* a justification of the established rules of contract law, an account of the conception of justice on which (in Hercules's opinion) contract law is based. Suppose that there are many well established rules relating to consideration in contract: rules holding that promises are not binding unless supported by consideration, that "past" consideration is not enough, and so forth. Hercules's theory of contract can scarcely treat all of these rules as mistakes, so his theory will have to link the bindingness of contracts to the existence of consideration. Yet it is surely conceivable that Hercules holds the moral viewpoint that *all* promises are binding and should be enforced, regardless of consideration. Is there then not a difference between Hercules's view of what morality requires and his view of what the law requires? Does it not follow that Dworkin's theory is perfectly consistent with the "separation of law and morals" that is asserted by legal positivists?

Let us consider various possible responses:

1. It might be argued that there is no conflict in our example between what morality requires and what the law requires, because morality requires respect for the law. The law should

109

not be simply *contrasted* with what morality requires, because the law itself affects our moral position. The trouble with *this* argument is that its claims are either unacceptable or they are consistent with legal positivism. If the argument is that we should *always* obey the law, it is unacceptable, because we do not usually regard the law as morally conclusive of what we should do. If the argument is that the law affects our moral position because it *may* be the case that we ought to obey the law in this instance, the argument is consistent with legal positivism. The positivist does not deny that we may have an obligation to obey the law, he merely holds that the question of the existence and scope of any such obligation is a separate question from the question of the content of the existing law.

2. It might be argued (following on from the first argument) that it is only the belief in a moral obligation to obey the law that explains the way in which we speak of the law as imposing duties and conferring rights. Something of this kind might be read into Dworkin's insistence that legal and other institutional rights are genuine moral or political rights. But the argument appears to involve saying that if, in a certain legal system, people have rights of ownership over slaves, these legal rights of ownership are genuine *moral* rights. Many find that consequence unacceptable.

3. It might be argued that, in working out his "soundest theory of law", Hercules has to develop a theory of why statutes and precedents are binding on him at all. This theory will form an integral part of Hercules's account of the existing law, but it will also be a direct expression of Hercules's views on the moral obligation to obey the law. For the legal positivist, we work out what the law *is*, and then ask the separate question of why we ought to obey it. But for Hercules, an account of why the black letter legal rules are binding on him forms a part of, and exerts a powerful influence on, his view of what the relevant legal principles and legal rights are. This is an interesting argument, and it receives an echo in the thought of some legal philosophers who see themselves as positivists. Neil MacCormick, for example, has doubted the possibility of separating a judge's account of the rule of recognition from his view of the "underpinning reasons" for the rule, *i.e.* his view of why he is bound by the rule at all. (See Neil MacCormick, *Legal Reasoning and Legal Theory* (1978), Chap. III.) But the majority of legal positivists would want to insist that questions of the

content of the doctrine of precedent, or the legal validity of statutes, are questions of law that can be settled quite independently of any issues about the moral bindingness of law in general.

Suppose that these and other arguments fail. We are then left with the following problem. Dworkin claims to have refuted legal positivism. The central tenet of legal positivism is the claim that the existence of a law is one thing, its moral merit or demerit is another: in other words, what morality requires is a separate question from what the law requires. But Dworkin's arguments appear to be consistent with this central tenet of legal positivism, since even for Hercules there is a gap between what the moral principles governing (for example) promises are, and what the legal principles are.

Dworkin's theory is consistent with legal positivism, however, only on a very narrow understanding of legal positivism. For legal positivists such as Austin, Bentham, Hart, and Kelsen do not *simply* claim that law is distinct from morality. They claim that law is distinct from morality *because* law consists of a body of commands, rules, norms, or other standards, which can be ascertained in a straightforward way by reference to *sources*. The exposition of the law should not, on the positivist view, be an inherently controversial task: it is simply a matter of establishing as a matter of fact which rules have actually been laid down by authorised sources. In Hart's theory, this general account is linked to the view that the whole point of having a rule of recognition is to provide standards of conduct which are publicly ascertainable, in the sense that you can work out what the law is without entering into any controversial moral judgments.

What Dworkin is attacking is this picture of law as ascertainable in a non-controversial manner. The construction of the "soundest theory of law" is a controversial task involving complex issues of moral and political theory. For example, if Hercules is faced by a hard case on frustration in the law of contract, he will need to ask questions such as the following: are the existing rules on frustration best justified by the theory that they are attempts to implement the will of the parties, or the theory that they are attempts to achieve a distributively just result in circumstances that were never contemplated by the parties? How far is it appropriate to attach overriding importance to the will of the parties given the existence of a redistributive welfare state committed to ideas of an egalitarian and paternalist nature?

These are not questions about Hercules's personal moral beliefs, but about the moral and political theory which best serves to justify these established legal rules. Hercules may be a libertarian of Nozickean cast, but in his judicial decisions, he has to take account of huge areas of the law which can be justified (if at all) only on non-libertarian grounds. At the same time, hard questions of law are not questions about what rules have been laid down, or what decisions were reached in earlier cases: if that was all there was to them, they would not be hard questions.

There are two quite different directions in which the general Dworkinian picture of legal reasoning could be developed. On one approach, Dworkin's rejection of legal positivism could be developed still further. The law could be portrayed as no less controversial than morality. Legal argument in hard cases could be viewed as a battle between rival ideological positions, with each side attempting to reinterpret the significance of the established rules and decisions. Indeed, by concentrating on the tendency of Dworkinian styles of legal reasoning to *unsettle* the black letter rules (as in *Riggs* v. *Palmer* itself), we might come to doubt whether it makes sense to employ a contrast between "established rules" and "controversial" principles. If we abandoned as illusory the foothold provided by established rules, the ideological debate in hard cases would be unconstrained: there would be nothing specifically "legal" about the arguments presented in hard cases, for they would simply be arguments of politics or morality.

The other direction in which the Dworkinian account could be developed tends to exploit common ground between Dworkin and the positivists. Hercules can certainly treat *some* rules as mistakes, and can even modify or reject established rules (on the ground that the principles supporting the rules are less weighty than other principles with which they conflict). But there are limits to how *extensively* he can do this: he cannot simply reject *all* the rules as mistakes, for he would then have no justification for treating as "legal" the principles he chose to rely on in rejecting these rules. On this view, therefore, the established black letter rules and decisions place genuine constraints on what Hercules can do. This means that his "soundest theory of law" will not be just the political theory he happens to approve of: it must represent the political theory which best serves to justify the established rules. Hercules must apply in hard cases, not his personal idea of justice, but the conception of justice that is implicit in the black letter rules of law: he must do justice *according to law*.

112

Seen from this perspective, the Dworkinian model of legal reasoning might be thought of as the fulfillment of an aspiration that is central to Hart's account of the rule of recognition. The rule of recognition exists to remedy the uncertainty of a régime of primary rules. But uncertainty still exists, for Hart, in hard cases, where the judge must exercise his discretion on extra-legal grounds. The Dworkinian account of legal reasoning shows how decision-making beyond the scope of the black letter rules can nevertheless be constrained by the law. Hercules must grapple with issues that are inherently controversial: but he is not simply thrown back on his personal moral beliefs and told to decide the case as he thinks best.

SELECTED READING

RONALD DWORKIN, *Taking Rights Seriously* (revised ed., 1978).

JOSEPH RAZ, "Legal Principles and the Limits of Law" (1972) 81 *Yale Law Journal* 823.

JOSEPH RAZ, "Professor Dworkin's Theory of Rights" (1978) 26 *Political Studies* 123.

DAVID LYONS, "Principles, Positivism and Legal Theory" (1977) 87 *Yale Law Journal* 414.

JOHN GRIFFITHS, "Legal Reasoning from the External and the Internal Perspectives" (1978) 53 *New York University Law Review* 1124.

A great many articles have been published discussing the work of Ronald Dworkin. A useful collection of some of the best of these is:

MARSHALL COHEN (Ed.), *Ronald Dworkin and Contemporary Jurisprudence*, (1984).

7. Fuller

Facts, values and purposes

In Chapter 5 I posed a problem in the following terms. Suppose that the Mafia gained control of the United Kingdom, even to the extent of removing the government and the existing apparatus of law and law enforcement. In place of these institutions, the Mafia established a new "legislature", and new "courts" which enforced Mafia decrees. Would this amount to a legal system?

Two approaches to the problem can be distinguished at the outset. On the one hand are theories that treat the concepts of law and legal system as having certain moral dimensions: on this view, a body of rules counts as a legal system only if, *inter alia*, it is aimed at the "common good" or the enforcement of justice. The other approach, which is characteristic of legal positivism, offers an account of law and legal systems that is purely formal in character. Legal systems are characterised, on this view, by the existence of certain types of institutional arrangement rather than by their underlying purpose or object. Thus, in Hart's theory, a legal system exists if there are officials who accept and apply a rule of recognition, and if the primary rules identified by the rule of recognition are obeyed by the bulk of the population.

The starting point for Fuller's theory is the insight that formal characterisations of human institutions independently of their purposes must be illusory and inadequate. Consider the way in which we would describe a human artifact such as a chair or a spoon to some alien being who had never encountered such objects. We might try to describe a chair (for example) in terms of its purely formal characteristics, without reference to its purpose. We would say something like "a chair consists of a more or less flat surface about 18 inches to three feet above the ground, usually supported by four legs, with a vertical surface rising from one edge of the flat horizontal surface". Such a description would be an uncertain guide, because chairs are so very various in appearance. Moreover the description would not really convey any understanding of what a chair is: to understand *that*, we would need to know what a chair is *for*. Once we understand what sitting is, and we know that a chair is for sitting on, we have a much better understanding of the concept of a chair.

The positivist attempt to describe legal systems in purely formal terms might be compared to the "formal" description of a chair. In both cases, the element of purpose is studiously neglected; and in both cases, the formal regularities exist for description only by virtue of the purpose that renders those formal features intelligible. In Fuller's opinion, the characteristic features of legal systems that have provided the focus for legal positivists exist *as* characteristic features only because they are related to the *purpose* of legal systems. Once we have a clear understanding of the purpose of legal systems, we will see that it is an inherently moral purpose, a moral aspiration. Thus an understanding of what law *is* cannot finally be separated from an understanding of what law ought to be, because understanding what law is involves a comprehension of moral aspirations that are implicit in the very concept of law itself.

Fuller's strategy of argument is as follows. He begins by identifying eight features of law that constitute minimum conditions, in the sense that a social formation that completely lacked any one of the eight would not normally be regarded as a legal system. He then seeks to demonstrate that the eight minimum conditions, taken collectively, amount to an intelligible moral ideal which can be seen as explaining the purposive features of law. Whereas complete failure to comply with any one of the eight results in something that is not a legal system at all, complete compliance with all of the eight conditions represents a moral aspiration that (by virtue of its connection with the minimum conditions) is implicit in the concept of law.

Legal positivists generally hold that there is a fundamental distinction between *facts* and *values*. The question of whether or not something is a legal system is a question of *fact*; the question of whether it is a good or bad legal system is a question of *value*. This suggests that two different sets of criteria are involved: one set of criteria is applied to determine whether something counts as a legal system, and the other (evaluative) set is applied to determine whether it is a good or bad legal system.

So far as a great many questions about the justice or injustice of the law is concerned, Fuller does not dispute the "two sets of criteria" view (if I may so style it). But he seeks to delineate a range of moral values where the fact/value distinction breaks down in its application to law. In relation to these values, we apply the same criteria in determining whether or not something counts as a legal system that we apply in determining whether it is a good or bad legal system. The eight minimum conditions represent, when perfectly complied with, a moral ideal towards which the law should strive to approximate.

The concept of law may once again be compared with spoons and chairs. We do not have one set of criteria for deciding whether something counts as a spoon and another set for deciding whether it is a good or a bad spoon. In both cases, the test is a purposive one. We understand what spoons are only by reference to their purpose. The formal features of spoons (the bowl, the handle, etc.) are intelligible only in the light of the spoon's purpose. A spoon that serves its purpose well is a good spoon. A spoon that serves its purpose badly is a bad spoon. At some point, the "spoon" may perform so badly that we would refuse to describe it as a spoon at all (a handle with no bowl, a bowl made of paper). Similarly with legal systems. There are purposes that render the formal features of legal systems intelligible. Unlike the purpose of spoons, the inherent purpose of legal systems is a recognisable moral aspiration. It amounts to an "inner morality of law".

The eight principles

In his principal book, *The Morality of Law*, Fuller tells an allegorical tale about a certain king "who bore the convenient, but not very imaginative and not even very regal sounding name of Rex". Rex wished to be a law-maker for his people. Unfortunately his efforts at law-making go astray in various ways, and he never succeeds in making any laws at all! I will not attempt to summarise Fuller's entertaining yarn. But the *point* of the story can be briefly explained, in two main points.

(1) Law-making is a purposive activity which can fail in its purpose. Like any other purposive activity, law-making requires attention to certain practical precepts related to the ultimate purpose of the activity. In relation to law-making there are eight such precepts. The basic object of law-making is to subject human conduct to the governance of rules. If this object is to be achieved

    (i)   there must be rules;
    (ii)   they must be prospective, not retrospective;
    (iii) the rules must be published;
    (iv) the rules must be intelligible;
    (v)   the rules must not be contradictory;
    (vi) compliance with the rules must be possible;
    (vii) the rules must not be constantly changing;
    (viii) there must be congruence between the rules as declared and as applied by officials.

(2) The eight precepts represent eight ways in which the enterprise of law-making can go astray. They point to eight minimum conditions for the existence of anything that we would regard as law or a legal system. For example, a system where *all* the rules were kept secret, or where *all* the rules were retrospective, would not normally be thought of as a legal system. Complete failure to comply with any one of the eight principles results in something that is not law at all.

Fuller describes his eight principles as an "inner morality of law", and this claim has generated much confusion. The majority of critics have been unable to see any justification for treating the eight principles as "moral". We shall consider these critical arguments later. For the present, we must pursue Fuller's argument a little further.

Fuller draws a distinction between what he calls "the morality of duty" and "the morality of aspiration". These two types of morality, or areas of morality, differ from each other both in logical structure and in rationale. The morality of duty is a matter of rules or standards which are regarded as obligatory. Compliance is seen as a duty, and one either complies or one does not; there are no questions of degree. The morality of aspiration is not structured in terms of *rules* but in terms of ideals: here, acting morally is a matter of striving to approximate to or emulate certain ideals or aspirations. Everything here is a question of degree. No one can expect to achieve completely the ideal requirements; but one must strive for the nearest approximation one can manage.

According to Fuller, the inner morality of law resembles a morality of aspiration. He means by this that the eight principles should not be thought of individually, as moral principles compliance with which is a duty; rather they should be thought of collectively as representing a moral aspiration for legal systems. No legal system can comply perfectly with all of the eight principles;

but, for every legal system, compliance should be pursued strenuously and seriously.

It is easy to see that Fuller's eight principles correspond to the idea of "the rule of law" (or at least to one aspect of that idea), long regarded as an important regulative ideal for Western legal systems. But Fuller is not simply trying to describe one possible value or ideal for legal systems: he is claiming that this ideal is implicit in the very concept of law itself. An understanding of what a "spoon" is involves an understanding of what spoons are for, and that in turn implies certain criteria for good and bad spoons. Similarly, to understand what "law" is we must have some understanding of the purpose of law and thus of the evaluative criteria that are relative to that purpose.

Law and purpose

"But", we may ask, "can't law have *any* purpose? Can't law be used for good purposes and bad?" This question reflects the criticism of Fuller's argument which has come to be most widely accepted, a criticism that was first formulated by Hart. Hart argued that Fuller had simply described eight principles for effective law-making. But law is an instrument that can be used for good purposes and for bad: its *efficacy* is not identical with *morality*. In Hart's view, Fuller had no real justification for calling the eight principles a "morality" of law. We might describe certain principles for effective poisoning (*e.g.* administer a dose that is large enough to kill, but not so large that it will cause vomiting; choose poisons which cannot be traced, etc.) but, Hart says, it would be absurd to describe these as an "inner morality of poisoning".

Is it true that the eight principles are mere principles of efficacy? First, we should notice that there is something question-begging in the description of them as principles of effective law-making. If Hart had said that they were principles of effective social control there would have been obvious objections to his claim. If social control is merely a matter of preventing widespread violence and revolutionary dissent, it is unlikely that Fuller's eight principles will be a good guide to the most effective techniques. A regime of terror where officials act unpredictably or on the basis of secret directives is much more likely to succeed in quelling opposition. Where clear rules are published, the citizen is given advance notice of those areas of conduct where he can act without fear of official interference. In the absence of such rules, any action that worries or annoys the officials is likely to be interfered with: the only way of avoiding interference is to maintain a compliant and totally conformist attitude and life style.

To say that the eight principles are principles of efficacy is therefore unhelpful, unless the object for which they are "effective" is more closely specified. The eight principles will not be a good guide to the effective techniques of mass coercion; and to describe them as principles of effective law-making begs the question of what law is and how it differs from organised coercion.

According to Fuller, law is "the enterprise of subjecting human conduct to the governance of rules". Stated baldly, this hardly describes anything that we would regard as an intelligible purpose. Suppose that you met someone who wanted to have rules that governed every aspect of human conduct: he had discovered, for example, that there were no rules governing the way people laced up their shoes, and he wanted to see this matter regulated as quickly as possible. When asked for a reason for having rules regulating the lacing up of shoes he simply replied "It is my purpose to subject human conduct to the governance of rules". Such a "purpose" would look more like a mental illness! What is required from Fuller is a much better account of why rules *matter*, of why it is a good thing to subject conduct to the governance of rules rather than (say) to the governance of terror and coercion or to no governance at all. Fortunately, such an account can be reconstructed from Fuller's arguments, and it casts considerable light on his notion of the eight principles as an "inner morality of law".

As we have seen, the moralities of duty and of aspiration are distinguished by their differing logical forms: one is framed in terms of obligatory rules, and the other in terms of ideals. But they are distinguished also by their point or rationale. The morality of aspiration fundamentally concerns the questions "How should I live? What goals and aspirations should I pursue?" It is in this sense that the morality of aspiration can be said to concern the "good life". But the questions posed by the morality of aspiration make sense only in a context where people can meaningfully formulate and pursue personal projects and ideals. If, for example, I am a slave whose every waking hour is absorbed in labour under the direction of others, it makes but little sense for me to ask "What goals and aspirations should I pursue?" Similarly, if social life is so lacking in order and regularity that I am likely at any moment to be murdered, imprisoned, or coerced, it makes little sense for me to formulate long term plans and projects for my life. In order for the morality of aspiration to have any application at all, it is necessary for there to be some degree of order and regularity in social life. This order and regularity is provided by the rules that comprise the morality of duty. Observance of the basic rules against killing, stealing, and so on, makes possible that degree of order and personal integrity that is an essential precondition for the meaningful confrontation of the demands of the good life, the morality of aspiration.

The eight principles described by Fuller resemble the morality of aspiration in their logical structure: they collectively represent an ideal towards which legal systems should strive but from which they will inevitably fall short. But the eight principles resemble the morality of duty in their rationale: their object is to provide that degree of regularity and order which is the context within which the morality of aspiration has application. This is the real meaning of Fuller's description of law as "the enterprise of subjecting human conduct to the governance of rules". Only when human conduct is subjected to the governance of rules can we (in Fuller's words) "rescue man from the blind play of chance and . . . put him safely on the road to purposeful and creative activity".

We are now in a position to see the fallacy that is involved in treating Fuller's eight principles as mere principles of efficacy. For us to speak meaningfully of efficacy, it must be possible to distinguish means from ends. Thus, there could be principles of effective poisoning because there is a definite end in view (a dead victim) and certain steps calculated to achieve that end (the right dose). But Fuller's eight principles are not related in this way to any independent end. Observance of the principles is valuable not because it is effective in the attainment of some goal, but because it is constitutive of that situation that we describe as "the rule of law". We value the rule of law because we value the projective capacities of men and women: we value "purposeful and creative activity" and we know that this is possible only within the context of a social order based on the observance of clear and declared rules.

Internal and external moralities

Fuller distinguishes between the internal (or "inner") morality of law, which is represented by his eight principles, and what he calls the external morality of law. The latter concerns the familiar question of whether the law is just or unjust, good or bad. But what does Fuller mean by the contrast between internal and external moralities?

The basic point is this. You and I may disagree about justice and about which laws would be just. There may or may not be ways of rationally resolving our dispute; but, as between our two views of justice, the concept of *law* will be neutral. The law could appropriately be used to implement either conception of justice. With the values represented by the eight principles, the position is different. These values are internal to the law in the sense that they form a part of the concept of law itself. We understand what law *is* only by reference to its purpose; and its purpose is an ideal state of affairs (the rule of law) represented by the eight principles. Every legal system will fall short of the ideal to some extent but (as the allegory of Rex demonstrates) too great a failure results in something that cannot be called a legal system at all. Law is not the only possible form of governance or social control: one might employ organised coercion, behavioural conditioning, or mediation and compromise, for example. But the use of law as against those other forms of ordering carries with it certain moral commitments. It carries a commitment to the idea of man as a rational purposive agent, capable of regulating his conduct by rules, rather than as a pliable instrument to be manipulated; and it carries a commitment to the values of the rule of law as expressed in the eight principles.

Because the eight principles are internal to the concept of law itself, the part that they can play in legal reasoning is quite different from the part played by values such as justice or equality. A judge who invokes some conception of justice as a justification for his decisions may be exposed to the criticism that his job is to apply the *law*, not to resolve controversial issues about justice which should be resolved democratically. But, since the eight principles form a part of the concept of law itself, the judge's duty to apply the law includes a duty to be guided by the eight principles. Thus, when lawyers and judges interpret laws in such a way as to make them clear and to remove apparent contradictions, they can justifiably claim to be exhibiting fidelity to law, rather than an unprincipled willingness to interfere with democratically enacted rules. Indeed Fuller insists that it is important not to confuse fidelity to law with mere deference to constituted authority. Fidelity to law involves a commitment to the eight principles, which therefore serve as general guidelines for the purposive activity of maintaining, applying and advancing a legal system.

Given the contrast between internal and external moralities, it should be clear that compliance with the eight principles does not guarantee that the law will be just. It is logically possible for a government to comply with the eight principles to a very high degree and nevertheless enact unjust laws. This is presumably what leads Hart to say that Fuller's inner morality of law is "compatible with very great iniquity". But Hart is mistaken if he imagines (as he seems to) that this demonstrates the inner morality to be no true morality at all. The fact that the rule of law is compatible with injustice does not demonstrate that it is not a genuine moral value. Imagine two régimes, A and B, both equally guilty of violating human rights of various kinds; régime A operates by clearly declared rules, consistently and scrupulously enforced, while régime B operates with the aid of retrospective legislation, unlawful acts of violence by officials, secret trials, secret laws, and so forth. Is there any moral value attaching to régime A's commitment to the rule of law? Clearly there is. Where the government acts in accordance with the eight principles it makes its behaviour both public and predictable. This means that the citizen who wishes to avoid official interference knows just how far he can go without meeting that interference; this provides the degree of order and regularity which is the necessary framework for purposeful and creative activity; moreover (and more importantly from the point of view of an evil régime) it gives the citizen areas of freedom which may be exploited in order to actively oppose the régime. These are familiar facts, and they reflect a belief that is as justifiable as it is widespread. Questions of due process and the rule of law are so far from being mere matters of "efficacy" that we ordinarily think of them as *constraints* on government power. But if Hart's arguments were correct, this approach would be fundamentally misconceived.

The fact is that compliance with the eight principles is logically consistent with the pursuit of evil aims in very much the same way that armed robbery is logically consistent with a scrupulous concern for paying one's debts. They are indeed logically consistent, but they are very unlikely to be found together. An evil régime which is likely to meet opposition from its subjects will not choose to operate through the rule of law. An evil régime that has the massive support of its populace (say, because it persecutes only a small minority group) may find it easier to comply with the eight principles; but even here such compliance would be problematic. Evil aims such as racist persecution could be pursued through the law, in Fuller's opinion, only by means of laws employing inherently vague and uncertain concepts of "race": this would violate the principles requiring clarity, and congruence between declared rule and official action. In any case, the eight principles make sense only in the context of a commitment to the value of man as a rational and purposive agent, a commitment that is likely to be absent in the worst varieties of tyranny.

If respect for the eight principles makes extreme forms of oppression improbable, it does not resolve the host of problematic questions about the justice of the law. Different views of justice are of course compatible with respect for the rule of law. But even here, Fuller argues, greater concern for the eight principles can help to resolve some controversial issues. There has, for example, been a long-running debate about the legal enforcement of personal sexual morality, laws against homosexuality being the most common example. Fuller argues that such laws should be removed from the statute book where they still exist because they lead to too great a deviation from the eight principles, particularly the principle requiring congruence between the declared rule and official action. Enforcement of such laws would be so sporadic and uncertain that a gulf would be created between the law as it appears in the books and as it is actually enforced.

Reciprocity, obligation and the rule of recognition

In examining Hart's legal theory, we noted the unusual emphasis that he places on the position of officials in the legal system. The foundation of legal validity, for Hart, is the rule of recognition, which is a rule accepted and applied by officials. We determine what the existing law is by reference to the facts of official behaviour.

Fuller completely rejects this approach. He accuses Hart of viewing law as a one way projection of authority, from the top down. According to Fuller, legality rests on a degree of reciprocity between ruler and ruled. Where officials and law-makers act in accordance with the eight principles, this degree of reciprocity is made possible. The law-maker in effect says "If you will comply with these rules, we guarantee that you will not be interfered with. We lay down these rules to regulate the behaviour of citizens and officials alike. If you comply, you can do so in the assurance that these are the rules by which your conduct will be judged."

The concept of legality is a curious one which has two rather different faces. On the one hand we tend to think of legality as a matter of the formal authorisation of official acts, the formal validity of rules and the like. On the other hand, "legality" seems to carry certain moral overtones: we regard legality as itself an important moral or political value. Hart's theory could be accused of focusing exclusively on the former aspect at the expense of the latter. Hart not only fails to *explain* why legality is seen as a precious value; he offers an account of the basis of legality (in official behaviour) that makes it look more like a matter of the streamlined exercise of power than a matter of the delicate balance between ruler and ruled.

It is one of the great strengths of Fuller's work that he casts light on such issues. Moreover, Fuller put forward a number of ideas in this general area which are profoundly provocative and could be developed much further. He argued that reciprocity was the basis of a legal system on a very wide front and that many legal rules are implicit in established practices and expectations: rather than being "made" (in accordance with an authorising rule of recognition), they are discovered. He suggested possible connections between the notion of reciprocity and the concept of an obligation, thereby provoking the thought that the normative vocabulary of law (rights, obligations etc.) may be explicable only by reference to the legal system's roots in reciprocity and he suggested that the basis of law and obligation in reciprocity may be a characteristic only of market societies, thus linking his work to a tradition of thought (on both right and left) that sees the development of non-market economies as incompatible with the rule of law.

SELECTED READING

LON FULLER, *The Morality of Law* (revised ed., 1959).

LON FULLER, *Anatomy of the Law* (1971).

H. L. A. HART, Book Review (1965) 78 *Harvard Law Review* 1281.

RONALD DWORKIN, "Philosophy, Morality and Law" (1965) 113 *University of Pennsylvania Law Review* 668.

ROBERT S. SUMMERS, *Lon L. Fuller* (1984).

Students should compare Fuller's view of law with that of Finnis. See:

FINNIS, *Natural Law and Natural Rights* (1980), Chaps. 1, 9, 10, 11 and 12.

Part Three

Rights

8. The Analysis of Rights

It is common to see a distinction drawn between "analytical jurisprudence" and "normative jurisprudence". Analytical jurisprudence is concerned with the formal analysis of concepts, in an effort to exhibit their logical structure and to reveal and refine conceptual distinctions. Normative jurisprudence is concerned to offer a theory about what is morally right and just, and therefore about the criteria by which the law should be evaluated. Thus the analytical jurisprudence of rights aims to answer the question of what it *is* to have a right: what exactly do we mean by "a right"? The normative jurisprudence of rights seeks to explain the moral foundation of rights and to answer the question "what rights do we actually have?"

This distinction is a conventional one and I shall use it in dividing the subject matter of this part of the book between the present chapter and Chapter 9. This chapter concerns the analytical jurisprudence of rights, while the following chapter is concerned with normative jurisprudence. But the distinction between analytical and normative inquiries is in fact a crude and misleading one. Our view of what exactly rights *are* is inevitably linked to our understanding of what rights people have. Moreover, it is possible to argue that the term "a right" bears a different meaning in different moral and political theories, in such a way that the whole analytical enterprise is cast into doubt. But my object is to expound well-established and influential theories. For that purpose, the conventional distinction will serve very well. Having noted my personal scepticism, I can leave the reader to reflect for him or herself on the problem.

Hohfeld

The American jurist Hohfeld is justly famous for a series of

129

analytical distinctions between different types of rights. Hohfeld's analysis makes a permanent contribution to clarity of thought and forms an excellent starting point for the theoretical discussion of rights. I do not propose, however, to explain all the aspects and refinements of the Hohfeldian scheme: rather, I shall single out a few key issues for discussion.

Hohfeld pointed out that, when lawyers talk about "rights", they use that term to refer to a number of quite different notions. These various types of "right" are ultimately reducible to four: (a) claim-rights (Hohfeld calls these simply "rights"); (b) liberties (Hohfeld used the term "privileges"); (c) powers; and (d) immunities. Other types of rights, such as the right of ownership, could be broken down by analysis into a combination of the four basic notions, which Hohfeld called the "lowest common denominators of the law". Each type of right is one aspect of a legal relationship between at least two persons. Claim-rights, liberties, powers and immunities are distinguished by what they imply about the legal position of the other party. (Hohfeld developed his analysis in relation to legal rights, but the bulk of the analysis can plausibly be applied to moral rights also.)

To say that X has a claim-right against Y implies that Y owes a duty to X. Thus if X has a claim-right that Y should pay him £100, this means that Y has a duty to pay X £100; if X has a claim-right that Y should not assault him, this means that Y has a duty not to assault X.

A liberty differs from a claim-right in that a liberty in X does not entail any duty owed by Y. If we say that X has a liberty as against Y to wear a hat, this means that Y has no claim-right that X should not wear a hat. In other words, if we say that X has a liberty to wear a hat we mean quite simply that X is under no duty *not* to wear a hat.

It should be carefully noted that all of the basic Hohfeldian rights (*i.e.* claim-rights, liberties, powers and immunities) must be thought of as rights against a specific person. Thus it can be misleading to simply speak of X having a liberty to wear a hat, for he may have such a liberty as against Y but not as against Z. If, for example, X has entered into a contract with Z whereby X promises not to wear a hat, he owes a duty to Z not to wear a hat, and Z has a claim-right that he should not wear a hat. But X still has a liberty as against Y, with whom he has no contract, and Y has no claim-right that X should not wear a hat.

Students are often confused by the fact that, in the Hohfeldian scheme, X's liberty does not entail any duty on the part of Y not to interfere. The fact that X has a liberty (as against Y) to wear a hat does not entail that Y has a duty not to interfere with X's hat-wearing. Y may be doing nothing wrong in stopping X from wearing a hat, *e.g.* if Y monopolises the world supply of hats and refuses to sell X one. Of course most of the ways in which Y might seek to prevent X from wearing a hat will involve an assault on X, and Y is under a duty not to assault X. But that duty is not the correlative of X's liberty, but of a separate claim-right enjoyed by X: the claim-right not to be assaulted. X's claim-right might be extinguished while his liberty survived. Suppose that X and Y were playing a game where X had to try to wear a hat while Y had to try to knock it off. X would then be waiving his normal claim-right not to be the victim of a (minor) assault: but his liberty to wear a hat would survive unimpaired, in that he still has no duty *not* to wear a hat, and Y has no claim-right that he should not wear a hat.

Rights such as the claim-right not to be assaulted have been described as providing a perimeter of protection for liberty. One of the law's most important and difficult tasks is to determine the forms and extent of that protection. For example, people have the liberty to operate commercial enterprises and to make profits. If X and Y have businesses which are in direct competition with each other, each will be seeking to expand at the expense of the other, and even to drive the rival out of business. The law must draw the line between legitimate competition and illegitimate interference. But there remains an area of free competition within which the liberties of X and Y are allowed to conflict. It is therefore a fallacy to argue that if X has a right to run a business, Y has a duty not to interfere with him. The argument would be valid only if by "a right" we meant a claim-right; but X enjoys only a *liberty* to run a business, and such a liberty does not entail any duty on Y's part. A claim-right is the correlative of a duty in the other party, but when we say that someone has a liberty to do an act we mean only that he is not doing anything wrong in performing the act: he violates no duty and infringes no claim-right.

Lawyers sometimes speak of rights when they mean neither liberties nor claim-rights, but what Hohfeld called "powers". A power is the ability to alter legal rights and duties, or legal relations generally. Thus one might have the power to make a will or to conclude a contract, each of these being an act that alters legal relations. Powers differ from claim-rights because they are not

131

correlative to a duty in someone else: Hohfeld describes them as being correlative to a "liability" in the other party, by which he means that party's liability to have his legal situation altered by an exercise of the power. Powers differ from liberties also. I may have the "power" (in Hohfeld's sense) to perform an act and yet not have the liberty to do so. In certain cases, for example, a non-owner can pass a good title to a bona fide purchaser for value. Such a person has the power to transfer title, since his acts will be legally effective in making the purchaser the owner of the goods. But the exercise of that power may still be a breach of duty: although effective in transferring title, it may still be a legal wrong. Since a liberty is the absence of a duty not to do the act, it is clear that the non-owner in such a case had the *power* to transfer, but not the *liberty* to do so. Imagine how confusing it would be if we did not possess the Hohfeldian vocabulary, but had to refer to both powers and liberties as rights. We would then have to say that the non-owner had the right to transfer, but did not have the right to transfer!

Immunities are essentially a matter of not being under a liability to have one's legal situation altered by the act of another. If X has a power, then Y is under a liability to have her legal position changed by having duties imposed on her, or rights conferred. Where X has such power, we may describe Y as enjoying an immunity.

The United States Bill of Rights is, in a sense, a Bill of Hohfeldian immunities. Such things as freedom of speech are, under that Bill, not simply liberties enjoyed by the citizen, but *immunities*, in that no legislature has the power to lawfully abridge the freedom by imposing duties not to speak freely. The exact limit of such immunities is, of course, a controversial matter. But American "civil liberties" differ from their British equivalents precisely in their status as immunities. British citizens may enjoy some degree of freedom of speech, but that enjoyment is precarious since it could at any time be abridged by Parliament. Freedom of speech in Britain is enjoyed as a Hohfeldian liberty, not an immunity.

The right of ownership is really a complex bundle of claim-rights, liberties, powers and immunities. An owner of land, for example, typically enjoys (*inter alia*) the claim-right that others should not trespass on his land, the liberty to walk upon his land, the power to transfer title to others, and an immunity against having his title altered or transferred by the act of another.

Correlativity of rights and duties

In Hohfeld's analytical scheme, claim-rights are correlative to duties in a very strict way. When we say that X has a claim-right of a certain kind, a part of what we mean (according to Hohfeld) is that Y owes a duty of some kind to X. Liberties are not correlative to duties: they are correlative to the *absence* of a claim-right, or what Hohfeld calls a "no-right" (thus if X has a liberty to wear a hat, Y has "no-right" that X should not wear a hat). Powers are correlative to liabilities (being liable to have one's legal position changed by the act of another) and immunities are correlative to disabilities (*i.e.* the inability to change another person's legal position).

The idea of strict correlativity between rights (*i.e.* claim-rights) and duties is a controversial one, and the controversy is important for two quite different sets of reasons, which we may summarise as follows:

1. If rights are strictly correlative to duties, then a person has established legal rights only insofar as there are established duties corresponding to those rights. The law on this account has a static appearance: it could be represented as a long list of duties. If, on the other hand, it makes sense to talk of established rights without established correlative duties, we may think of the law as imposing duties, and perhaps creating new duties, *in order to protect* established rights. On this account, there may at any one time be established legal rights which are inadequately protected by legal duties: such rights provide a legal reason for creating new legal duties. Seen from this perspective, the law is not static but has an inner dynamic of its own. It is not a long list of duties that is added to whenever moral and policy considerations make this desirable: new duties may be recognised as a response to specifically legal considerations, in the attempt to give better legal protection to established legal rights.

2. Politicians and others make frequent use of the concept of rights. People are said to have rights of this and that kind, and rights are generally regarded as a "good thing". But if rights (in this case moral, rather than legal, rights) are correlative to duties, such claims are always open to the question "on whom do the correlative duties rest?" People are much more willing to assert the existence of rights to various amenities than they are to ascribe specific duties. Moreover, if rights are correlative

133

to duties, we may feel that they are not necessarily an unqualified good: for if rights entail duties, they entail greater restrictions on freedom. If therefore we believe that freedom is a "good thing" we will not wish to see an unlimited expansion in people's rights (meaning, I repeat, "claim-rights").

The most interesting arguments against the strict correlativity of rights and duties have been offered by Neil MacCormick. MacCormick's principal argument is that the idea of correlativity obscures the fact that duties are imposed in order to protect rights: the existence of a right is a justifying reason for imposing a duty. The claim that rights are strictly correlative to duties obscures this point, because it involves holding that part of what we mean by saying that X has a right is that Y already has a duty: thus the rights cannot be a reason for imposing a duty on Y. Indeed, in MacCormick's analysis, rights can be protected in other ways than by the imposition of duties. They may be protected by the conferment of Hohfeldian liberties or powers, or by the imposition of Hohfeldian disabilities on other persons. A follower of Hohfeld would insist that, when we speak about rights, we should make it clear whether we mean claim-rights, liberties, powers or immunities. But, according to MacCormick, we may speak of rights without this kind of discrimination because, at their most basic level, rights are the justifying reasons for the creation of Hohfeldian claim-rights, liberties, powers and immunities: the latter concepts represent various legal devices for the protection of rights.

MacCormick's other argument is less interesting, but deserves mention. He points out that statutes may sometimes confer rights without imposing duties on anyone. The example he offers is section 2(1) of the Succession (Scotland) Act 1964, which provides that an intestate's children shall have the right to the whole of the intestate estate. Here there is no duty on anyone until an executor has been appointed; vesting of the right is therefore temporally prior to vesting of the duty. Moreover, a child of the intestate has a preferential right to be confirmed as executor by virtue of his right to the estate. In MacCormick's view, this statutory provision is an example of (1) a right being temporally prior to a duty; (2) a right being the reason for imposing a duty (*i.e.* the child's right is a reason for his being appointed executor); and (3) a duty being borne by the bearer of the "correlative" right.

At first this example does seem to pose intractable problems for the correlativity thesis! But on reflection, the difficulties will be seen to be less formidable. After all, we are quite familiar with the idea of the duties of an office, and we do not think of such duties as springing in and out of existence each time the office holder changes. We think of the duties as attaching to the continuing office, not the changing holder of the office. Thus we may think of the right created by section 2(1) of the Succession (Scotland) Act 1964 as being correlative to the duty borne by the office of executor. The right is thus not temporally prior to the duty. Similarly there is nothing odd in speaking of an office holder owing a duty to himself in his private capacity: a wages officer might have the duty of paying all the firm's employees, including himself. Nor does MacCormick's example present an instance of a right being the reason for imposing a duty: the child's right is a reason for appointing the child to an office that carries a duty, not a reason for creating the duty.

Will and interest theories

There has been a long running dispute between theories of rights that connect rights with freedom or "the will", and theories that see rights as concerned with interests more generally. The majority of combatants in this dispute have tended to assume the correlativity of rights and duties, and it will be convenient to begin with arguments that take that assumption as a starting point. More recently, as we shall see, Neil MacCormick has offered a version of "interest" theory that rejects the correlativity of rights and duties.

In its classical form, the interest theory of rights claims that a right is an interest which is protected by the imposition of a duty on another person or persons. More precisely, a right-holder is the intended beneficiary of a duty. Thus, if I have a duty to pay you £100, you have a corresponding right because and insofar as you are the intended beneficiary of my duty. If I have a duty not to assault you, you have a corresponding right for the same reason.

It is not enough for the right-holder to be a beneficiary of the duty if he is not the *intended* beneficiary: it must be the object of the duty (or the legal or moral rule that imposes the duty) to benefit the right-holder. For example, the manufacturers of motor-cycle crash helmets no doubt benefit from a law compelling the wearing of helmets. But it was not the object of the law to benefit such manufacturers, and we would not speak of such manufacturers as having a right that people should wear helmets. The rights of helmet manufacturers in this regard do not differ from those of other members of the public.

It is not always easy to determine who the intended beneficiaries of a duty are, and this inevitably introduces a degree of uncertainty into the language of rights, when analysed from the point of view of the interest theory. But a more serious objection to the interest theory points out that the intended beneficiary of a duty is not invariably thought of as the holder of a correlative right. Suppose that you and I enter into a contract whereby I promise to perform certain services for you if you will pay £100 to a third party, X. In this situation, the intended beneficiary of your duty to pay £100 is X. However, in English law, X does not have a right that you should pay the money: I alone have that right. I have a right that you should pay X £100, but X has no similar right. But what exactly does this mean?

The will theory explains the problem in the following way. In some cases, the enforcement of a duty is made conditional on an exercise of will by someone other than the person who has the duty. In such cases, the party whose will is made decisive is spoken of as having a right. Duties imposed by contract, or by the law of tort, for example, can generally be waived by the parties to whom the duties are owed. If you are under a contractual obligation to me, and I choose not to enforce that obligation, no one else can complain about your non-performance of the duty. Duties imposed by the criminal law, on the other hand, cannot be waived in this way. If you steal from my house, and I decide not to prosecute, other people (such as the police) may nevertheless decide that you should be punished and may proceed to prosecute you. It is because powers of waiver exist in civil law but not in criminal law that we generally speak of the former but not the latter as conferring rights. It is because a contractual duty to pay money to a third party is subject to powers of waiver enjoyed by the other contracting party, but not enjoyed by the third party beneficiary, that we speak of the former but not the latter as possessing a right. So argues the will theory.

As I have already mentioned, a powerful version of the interest theory of rights, and an attack on the will theory, has been offered by Neil MacCormick. The will theory, as I have explained it so far, presupposes the correlativity of rights and duties, since it treats a right as being a power of waiver over someone else's duty. Part of MacCormick's attack on the will theory is his attack on the notion of correlativity, and his arguments on this issue have already been examined. The version of interest theory offered by MacCormick

136

does not presuppose the correlativity of rights and duties. Rather, it treats a right as a reason for imposing a duty, or for providing some other form of protection for the interests of the right bearer. Thus MacCormick holds that when we ascribe a right to someone (say, a right to a minimum level of pay) we are saying that the interest represented by that right (*i.e.* the interest in receiving the pay) is an interest which ought to be protected. It will be seen from this that, even if MacCormick *has* provided a convincing case against the correlativity of rights and duties, it is by no means clear that he has provided a convincing alternative. For MacCormick's rights appear to be correlative to "oughts" even if they are not correlative to "duties": what is the difference between saying that we "ought" to provide certain levels of pay, and saying that we have a duty to do so?

MacCormick has two arguments against the will theory which are quite independent of his attack on correlativity. The first argument concerns restrictions on the power of the right holder to waive or alienate his right, and the second argument concerns the difficulty that the will theory has in accommodating children's rights.

The will theory considers the essence of a right to be a power of waiver over someone else's duty. But, MacCormick argues, the law sometimes restricts powers of waiver, and such restrictions are not usually regarded as limiting or abolishing our rights: more commonly they are seen as attempts to strengthen our rights. Two types of cases should be distinguished:

1. In some cases an act continues to be unlawful even though the "victim" consents to it, *e.g.* murder and grievous bodily harm. In other cases, consent is a good defence, *e.g.* minor assaults in the course of a game.
2. In some cases people are given rights and are deprived of the power to contract out of the right. This is commonly the case with rights conferred on employees.

MacCormick argues that in both types of case, the will theory leads to paradoxical conclusions. In the first type of case, the will theory requires us to say that we have rights not to be assaulted in a minor way (since here we have a power of waiver) but no right not to be grievously assaulted (since here we have no power of waiver). In the second type of case, the will theory requires us to say that legislation preventing employees from contracting out of their rights *restricts* those rights, by restricting the scope of the power of waiver.

But such legislation would obviously be thought of as strengthening the employee's rights.

The second type of case can be dealt with relatively easily. MacCormick here confuses the power of waiver over the enforcement of the duty (which, according to the will theory, is the essence of a right) with the power to alienate the right. The right itself is a power to demand that the employer performs his obligations, including the power to sue or not as the employee chooses. By prohibiting the employee from contracting out of his rights, we do not *restrict* his power of waiver: we merely ensure that he continues to possess it.

The first type of case is more complex as it hinges on the view that we take of the criminal law. The criminal law (unlike the civil law) is not usually thought of as conferring rights. Of course, part of the object of the criminal law is the *protection* of rights, but these rights are conferred either by morality (*e.g.* in the case of the right not to be assaulted) or by civil law (in the case of property rights). It is not at all clear, however, that the protection of rights is the predominant concern of those areas of criminal law to which MacCormick directs his attention. Laws punishing acts of violence perpetrated on consenting adults are not best seen as protecting the rights of those adults. In some cases they are concerned to punish activities which are regarded as immoral but not as violating anyone's rights, *e.g.* MacCormick uses the example of the flagellation of (or by) a prostitute, which is illegal irrespective of the "victim's" consent. In other cases, the acts are punished in a paternalistic spirit, to protect the "victim" from his or her own folly in consenting to the illegal act, *e.g.* euthanasia. It is doubtful if paternalism of this kind is best interpreted as a protection of the party's rights.

So much for MacCormick's argument concerning restrictions on the power of waiver. His other principal argument concerns the rights of children.

According to the will theory, "a right is an option or power of waiver over the enforcement of a duty" and the right-holder is the person who can demand performance or waive it, who can choose to sue or not sue. Such powers are not generally exercised by children. Where duties are owed to children, the enforcement of those duties is not left at the discretion of the child. In the case of legal rights, the power of waiver or enforcement rests in the hands of the child's parent or guardian. MacCormick argues that these facts should lead exponents of the will theory to conclude that children do not have any rights. But that conclusion, MacCormick suggests, would be preposterous: we know that children have rights, therefore the will theory must be false.

H. L. A. Hart defended the will theory in a number of important papers which preceded MacCormick's work. Hart appreciated the problem with children's rights and draws the following conclusions. So far as moral rights go, Hart accepted that it is a mistake to ascribe rights to small babies, at least. The moral requirements on our conduct towards such infants are not based on respect for the infant's will, and therefore are not a matter of respect for rights (presumably Hart believed that, with older children, there are some areas of life where the child's will is controlling and where, therefore, the child can be spoken of as having rights). This conclusion should not be dismissed too quickly. Respect for rights is not the only possible basis for morality: there are duties of humanity, and moral requirements of love and compassion, to which the notion of "rights" is irrelevant.

In relation to legal rights, Hart adopted the conventional view that, in exercising powers of waiver, the parent or guardian is exercising the child's rights on behalf of the child. The fact that the parent or guardian is exercising the *child's* rights and not his own is borne out, Hart argues, by two features of the situation: (i) what the parent or guardian can do in exercising the power is determined by what the child could have done if *sui juris*, and (ii) when the child becomes *sui juris* he can exercise the powers without any need for an assignment of them. These features show that the powers are regarded as belonging throughout to the child, though exercised by another during the period of immaturity.

Legal and moral rights

Most of the analytical issues we have discussed above can be applied to both legal rights and moral rights. But what exactly is the relationship between legal and moral rights? This is really just another way of asking about the relationship between law and morality, which is an issue discussed in Chapters 5, 6 and 7 above. But it may be useful at this point to outline a couple of alternative positions.

The central question may be expressed in this way: "Is a legal right really a kind of moral right, or is a legal right something utterly different from a moral right?"

Legal positivist theories such as that of Hart would draw a clear distinction between legal and moral rights. Law is seen by these theories as a body of rules laid down by courts and legislatures. In reporting the content of these rules we make use of the concepts of "right" and "duty". But such concepts do not carry with them any element of moral approval: they are simply technical devices for expressing the content of positive legal rules.

We have seen that Hart is not altogether successful in achieving his separation of law and morality. He concedes that concepts such as "right" and "duty" are appropriately used only from an "internal point of view", and that looks very much like a point of view of moral approval. We may therefore be tempted by a more traditional standpoint which argues that law cannot be spoken of as conferring rights and imposing duties unless it has some moral claim on our conduct. This latter view does not mean that law can only confer rights if it is just. Even if the law is unjust there may be strong moral reasons for complying with it: organised society needs publicly ascertainable rules which are not at the mercy of each individual's personal views of justice, and we should therefore be prepared to comply with such rules even when we consider them to be unjust. Similarly the requirement of formal justice, that like cases be treated alike, may confer on individuals a right to a certain decision from a court of law even if that decision would be wrong as a matter of abstract justice. On this type of approach, therefore, legal rights may be thought of as a variety of *moral* rights: they are the moral rights that we have as a result of the existence of legal institutions such as bodies of publicly ascertainable rules and courts committed to the principle of formal justice.

SELECTED READING

W. N. HOHFELD, *Fundamental Legal Conceptions* (1919).

GLANVILLE WILLIAMS "The Concept of Legal Liberty" in R. S. SUMMERS (Ed.), *Essays in Legal Philosophy* (1968).

H. L. A. HART, *Essays on Bentham* (1982), Essays 7 and 8.

NEIL MACCORMICK, *Legal Rights and Social Democracy* (1982), Chap. 8.

NEIL MACCORMICK, "Rights in Legislation" in P. M. S. HACKER and J. RAZ (Eds.), *Law, Morality and Society* (1977).

T. CAMPBELL, *The Left and Rights* (1983).

A. WHITE, *Rights* (1984).

9. The Foundation of Rights

For some theories of law, such as that of Ronald Dworkin, rights occupy the central role in legal reasoning. Moral questions of law, on this view, raise the issue of what rights we have, and legal reasoning must proceed on the basis of some theory about how people come to have any rights at all. For other theories, such as that of Hart, the notion of a right plays a somewhat more subordinate role. Legal reasoning, according to Hart, is essentially concerned with the interpretation and application of legal *rules*: we speak of rights and obligations only in expressing conclusions about the scope, and implications for specific cases, of rules.

Even when legal theories do not give pride of place to the concept of a right in their accounts of legal reasoning, they tend to give considerable importance to the concept in the realm of moral argument. In the twentieth century it has become increasingly common to assume that any acceptable moral or political theory must be framed in terms of individual rights, and claims about the existence of such rights proliferate in popular discussions as well as in philosophical writings. The rapid growth of law relating to the international protection of human rights is only one indication of the importance now attached to rights and the near universality of appeals to rights.

The popularity of the concept of human rights in current politics is, in fact, somewhat anomalous. For the most widely influential moral and political theory of the last hundred years (at least in the West) has certainly been utilitarianism: and it is widely believed amongst philosophers that utilitarianism cannot accommodate any notion of individual or human rights. A concern to maximise the general welfare must treat all individual interests as subject to the calculus of utility. Freedom of speech, freedom from arbitrary arrest, and so on (pick your favourite human right) will be protected by the utilitarian only where that will maximise welfare overall. But the notion of a *right* seems to involve the idea that the right should be

protected under all but (perhaps) the most exceptional circumstances: rights should not be overridden every time that a marginal
increase in welfare is thereby to be achieved. We must therefore ask
the following questions: is a commitment to individual rights truly
inconsistent with utilitarianism? If so, what type of moral theory is
implied by a belief in basic human rights? And, on any such theory,
just what rights do we have?

Some theorists have argued that we should only speak of rights
where there are established positive rules conferring those rights.
Such rules might be black letter rules of law, or widely accepted
rules of social morality. A number of different strands of thought
contribute to these "positivist" theories of rights (as I shall call
them). Some such theories are varieties of rule-utilitarianism, and
will be discussed as such in the next section. Other positivist theories
of rights develop the idea that asserting a right is quite different
from suggesting that something would be on the whole desirable or
good: rights have special normative force. This special normative
force, it is argued, is the result of invoking rules that we already
accept and are committed to, rather than simply appealing to
general moral considerations. But a third type of positivist theory,
often believed to be particularly powerful and compelling, points to
the uncertainty of claims about non-positive rights, and the
unresolvability of discussions about rights. Only if we restrict the
idea of rights to rights conferred by positive rules (this approach
argues) can the concept of a right have any definite content and
value. If people are to claim "rights" that are not recognised or
conferred by any positive or actually accepted rules, their claims are
vacuous.

Yet, is there any reason for thinking that claims about non-
positive moral rights are uncertain *by comparison with other moral
arguments*? Claims about rights appear to be unusually problematic
and uncertain only if we contrast them with arguments of utility,
since such arguments *purport* to treat moral issues as resolvable by
reference to empirical criteria (what will *actually* maximise welfare?).
The idea that talk about rights is peculiarly uncertain thus leads us
back once more to the problem of the relationship between rights
and utility. This relationship is really the heart of the matter. For, if
it is true that rights in some sense *override* utility, we must ask why
that is so. Why should the freedom of speech of an individual (for
example) override considerations of the general welfare? Why
should we be prevented from making most people, on balance,
better off, simply because achieving that object would involve some

interference with the rights of perhaps a single individual? In attempting to answer these questions we are inevitably led to consider the whole nature and basis of rights.

Rights and utility

Is it really the case that a utilitarian cannot consistently support the idea of individual rights? We saw in the last chapter that Neil MacCormick analyses the concept of a right in the following way. According to him, when we say that someone has a right (say) to freedom of speech we mean that their interest in speaking freely ought to be protected. Suppose that a utilitarian adopted this analysis of rights. He might then hold that whether or not a certain interest ought to be protected should be determined by reference to the principle of utility. When, in the interests of the general welfare, that interest truly *ought* to be protected, he could speak of the individual as having a corresponding right. In this way, it might be argued, individual rights can be shown to be entirely consistent with utilitarianism.

The problem with this type of approach can be summed up in two points:

1. it fails to account for the relative *stability* of rights, and
2. it fails to explain the common belief that rights can, in some instances, override considerations of the general welfare.

A utilitarian might well believe that the protection of freedom of speech will always be dependent upon the utilitarian calculus: a change in circumstances could easily lead to the conclusion that, in this or that instance, it would maximise welfare to restrict freedom of speech, *e.g.* censoring the press in time of war. On the analysis we have presented so far, the utilitarian would have to conclude that, in such cases, the right to freedom of speech no longer existed. Yet we do not think of rights as coming and going with our changing calculations of utility: if people have a *right* to speak freely, that right does not cease to exist the moment it comes into conflict with the general welfare. Indeed, many people would suggest that it is precisely when they conflict with the general welfare that rights become truly important, for they should be understood, not as steps on the way to the maximisation of utility, but as constraints that limit what can permissibly be done in pursuit of utility.

The utilitarian might respond to this argument by questioning the whole idea that rights are stable, immune from fluctuating considerations of utility, and of such great importance that they constrain the pursuit of utility. Although philosophers tend to take this idealised view of rights for granted (or have done in recent years), such a view is much less common in ordinary legal and political life. For example, the Universal Declaration of Human Rights states that "rights and freedoms" shall be subject to limitations that are necessary for the general welfare, and such expressed limitations are common in international and constitutional documents protecting human rights. The utilitarian may take these qualifications as reflecting the truth of his view that individual rights are important only when and insofar as their protection tends to increase welfare generally.

Alternatively, the utilitarian can concede that rights do appear to have a degree of stability and an overriding quality that is impossible to explain on the basis of an "act-utilitarian" position. But these features of rights *can* be accommodated (he might argue) by a "rule-utilitarian" theory. (For the contrast between act-utilitarianism and rule-utilitarianism, see Chapter 1).

The rule-utilitarian holds that, in many instances, the general welfare will not be maximised if everyone seeks to act on the basis of the principle of utility. This may seem paradoxical at first glance, but the point is that, where everyone attempts to apply the principle of utility directly to his action, and chooses an action that will itself have the best consequences, the result may fail to maximise welfare for two reasons:

1. people will be unable to co-ordinate their actions satisfactorily, and so will not achieve the increase in welfare that is the product of co-ordination,
2. people will make mistakes in applying the principle of utility, and will choose actions that do not in fact maximise welfare.

These two problems are best solved, according to the rule-utilitarian, by adopting certain rules of conduct which should be followed without direct regard to considerations of utility. We should choose the *rules* that will maximise welfare, and should then comply with those rules without asking, in each case, whether our individual *actions* will maximise welfare. Thus, suppose that we believe that freedom of speech generally tends to maximise welfare: it is itself an important source of satisfaction, it tends to expose errors and corruptions, and it encourages intelligence and self-reliance amongst citizens generally. We might regard this as a good argument for adopting a rule conferring a *right* to speak freely. Such a right would be conferred solely for its instrumental value in maximising welfare. But it ought to be respected even when, in the particular case, the speech will not maximise welfare but will harm it. In this way the rule-utilitarian believes that he can account for both the *stability* of rights and their apparently *overriding* quality. Rights are stable and not subject to every marginal shift in the calculus of utility because and in so far as they are based on accepted rules (it will be noticed that many rule-utilitarian theories of rights are also positivist in character, given the idea that rights are conferred by positive or accepted rules). Rights appear to *override* considerations of utility because we should be prepared to respect the rights enjoyed under accepted rules even when, in the individual case, it would maximise welfare to infringe the right.

The objections to this argument are the general objections to rule-utilitarianism outlined in Chapter 1 (and students should refer back to that chapter). They may be summarised in the following points:

1. If the whole point of the rules is to maximise utility, what reason has a person for complying with the rules when he *knows* that, in this instance, observance of the rule will not maximise utility?
2. Because of the preceding point, the rules could be regarded as binding in all cases only by someone ignorant of their basis in considerations of utility. Thus the rule-utilitarian would have to adopt a form of "Government House utilitarianism" which encourages the populace to obey rules whilst keeping them in ignorance of the rational basis for those rules.
3. When the rule-utilitarian speaks of "rules" he may mean actually accepted or positive rules, in which case his theory will have a conservative and positivistic cast; or he may mean ideal or hypothetical rules, in which case his theory is threatened with vacuousness.

In any case, we should be suspicious of utilitarian claims to the effect that respect for individual rights will in fact maximise welfare. One could make out an equally plausible case for the claim that welfare can be maximised only by ignoring individual rights. The consequences of our actions are infinite and are impossible to predict with confidence: the result is that everything and nothing can be justified by an appeal to consequences.

Rights and freedom

We commonly distinguish between what people have a right to do, and what is the right thing for them to do. Thus we may say of someone that he ought not to go out and get drunk every night, but that nevertheless he has a right to do so. What is the significance of this distinction?

One plausible suggestion is that what rights people have determines the circumstances in which they may justifiably be interfered with. Even if Jane is wrong to drink so heavily we ought not to forcibly prevent her from drinking, because she has a right to decide for herself what she will do. But forcible intervention (or legal restriction) might be justified to prevent Jane from driving when drunk, because then her actions threaten to infringe the rights of others. By reflecting on examples of this kind, we may be led to conclude that rights mark out an area within which each person may act freely, whether or not his actions are approved of by others. A person's actions may be bad, foolish or wicked, but it is only when he violates or threatens to violate the rights of others that his freedom may be interfered with.

This general analysis suggests that every right is, in one way or another, a right to freedom. The analysis thus connects very closely with the will theory of rights, discussed in the last chapter. If rights mark out an area of freedom for each person, they mark out an area within which that person's will is decisive. Applying Hohfeld's scheme, we may see how this could be true of claim-rights, liberties, powers and immunities. Claim-rights make the enforcement of another's duty depend on one's exercise of will. Liberties *are themselves* areas of freedom unrestricted by duty. Powers make the alteration of legal relations dependent on one's will; and immunities ensure that it is only by one's own act (if at all) that one's legal relations may be altered.

Not every legal system, and not every social morality, employs the concept of a right. Hart has pointed out that ancient Greek contained no word that can be translated as meaning "a right". If we think of rights as marking out an area of freedom, it follows that only societies attaching some overriding importance to freedom will employ the concept of a right. If our morality is exclusively concerned with the quality of people's lives, we will evaluate conduct as good or bad, but not in terms of rights. Rights make sense only in the context of a belief that people should *lead their own lives*, whether those lives are good or bad, wise or foolish. Only when they threaten, by their conduct, to interfere with the freedom of others should people be restrained by the law.

The upshot of the argument is sometimes expressed by the claim that all rights are derived from a basic right to equal liberty. We have a basic right to equal liberty in the sense that we have a right to do as we please except where our actions interfere with the similar ability of others to do as *they* please. All other rights (property rights, rights enjoyed under contracts, etc.) are derived, directly or indirectly, from that basic right.

The idea of a basic right to equal liberty may seem an attractive one, but it poses serious problems. To begin with, there are problems in determining what exactly counts as an interference with freedom. Clearly the coercion or physical restraint of another interferes with his freedom, but what of causing him pain and suffering? If we say that he has a right to be "free" from pain we are no longer using the concept of freedom in the sense of freedom of action. Once we are prepared to speak of "freedom *from*" this or that, rather than simple freedom of action, we open the door to the legitimation of any laws whatever, since *anything* can be described as "freedom from" its opposite (a full belly is "freedom from hunger"; a quiet environment is "freedom from noise"). Interpreted in this way freedom ceases to be a distinct value, and simply becomes an empty catch-all under which any political values may be subsumed.

On the other hand, if we interpret freedom more restrictively, we will find it impossible to justify many of the laws that we currently take for granted. Henry Sidgwick doubted whether property rights and contractual rights could be justified by reference to a basic right to equal freedom. Even if we are less sceptical than Sidgwick on this question, we must at least concede that rights to welfare cannot be justified in any obvious way by a basic right to freedom. Rights to welfare are not rights not to be interfered with, but rights to be positively assisted. Such rights could have no place in a scheme based on the basic right to equal freedom.

Rights as trumps

One of the most interesting philosophical theories of rights to be offered in recent years is that of Ronald Dworkin. Dworkin's basic idea is that a right is a political trump which overrides considerations of the general welfare in their bearing on political decision making. When governments and legislatures are making decisions about the enactment of new laws, the allocation of money, or the exercise of governmental powers, the fact that a particular decision will advance the general welfare better than any alternative is generally a good reason for taking that decision. But, Dworkin argues, this is not so where the contemplated decision would interfere with individual rights. When we ascribe a right to someone, such as a right to freedom of speech, we are in effect holding that that person ought not to be interfered with, in respect of his freedom of speech, even if such interference would be in the interests of the general welfare. Rights may be restricted in order to demarcate their boundaries in relation to other, competing, rights. Thus the right of free speech comes into conflict with the right to be protected in one's reputation: a frontier between the two rights must be defined, and such a frontier is worked out in detail in the law of defamation. Rights may also, in some cases, be restricted in order to avoid very serious damage to the general welfare, or to achieve very large gains: thus, freedom of speech may be restricted in wartime in order to avoid defeat by the enemy. Rights vary in importance, and the power of a right to trump considerations of welfare depends upon how important the right is. But every right must have some power to override considerations of welfare, or it would not be a genuine right. The prospect of a marginal increase in the general welfare can never be a good reason for restricting or interfering with someone's rights.

Employing this analysis, Dworkin rejects the idea of a basic right to liberty. If people had such a right, it would mean that their liberty could not be restricted on purely utilitarian grounds. But we regularly enact laws that are regarded as justified by the fact that they increase the general welfare, and such laws place restrictions on liberty. Dworkin gives the example of a law making Lexington Avenue into a one way street. A law of this kind is justified by its effects on the general welfare, but it nevertheless restricts liberty. If people had a general right to liberty, such a law could not be justified. In fact, Dworkin argues, people have no such general right. Rather than a general right to liberty, people have rights to certain specific *liberties*, such as freedom of conscience and freedom from arbitrary arrest. (It will be recalled that a similar rejection of a general right to liberty in favour of rights to specific liberties underlies Rawls's First Principle of Justice).

If rights are thought of as political trumps that override

considerations of the general welfare, they clearly require a justification. Why should the interests of an individual in freedom of speech (for example) take priority over the general welfare? After all, in forming a view of what will advance the general welfare, the interest in free speech has already been taken account of and weighed against other, competing interests. The effect (on Dworkin's analysis) of saying that free speech is a right, is to place the interest in free speech above the social balance of one interest against another. Why should any interest be given that type of priority?

To understand Dworkin's answer to this question we must begin by reflecting on why utilitarianism is an appealing political theory at all. Why does it seem somehow obvious that governmental decisions should aim to increase the general welfare? Dworkin believes that the moral appeal of utilitarianism rests on the fact that, in forming a judgment about the general welfare, each person's interests are taken account of equally. In fact, Dworkin holds, both utilitarianism, and Rawls's *Theory of Justice*, derive their moral and intellectual appeal from an idea that is silently presupposed by both of them: the idea that people have a basic right to equal concern and respect when political decisions that will affect them are being taken. In utilitarianism this basic right finds expression in the idea that each person counts for one, and no person counts for more than one, in the calculus of utility. In Rawls's theory, the basic right to equal concern and respect finds expression in the required unanimity of the choice of principles of justice in the original position.

We have already seen how Rawls's argument leads to the conclusion that individuals have certain rights that are not subject to the calculus of utility. Dworkin believes that, if we take seriously the idea that utilitarianism is founded on a right to equal concern and respect, we will be led to the conclusion that a belief in individual rights, with power to trump considerations of welfare, is a more satisfactory expression of that basic foundation than is utilitarianism in its classical Benthamite form.

Dworkin's argument focuses on modern versions of utilitarianism that I described in Chapter 1 as "preference utilitarianism" (though his argument could probably be adapted to fit other forms of utilitarianism that take "happiness" or "pleasure" as their maximand). Preference utilitarianism requires us to maximise the extent to which people can satisfy their preferences. But what preferences are to count for this purpose?

149

Dworkin proposes that only "personal" preferences should count, and "external" preferences should be ignored. A personal preference is a preference about what I do or get; an external preference is a preference that *I* have about what *other* people do or get. For example, a white racist might want to have a big shiny car and lots of money, and he might also want blacks *not* to have big shiny cars and lots of money. The former preference is a personal preference, the latter is external. Dworkin's argument is that, in arriving at conclusions about the general welfare, we should ignore external preferences. Suppose that blacks and racists all want big shiny cars. Since there is a limit to the number of cars available, these preferences will compete with each other. Not everyone who wants a car will get one. There is nothing unjust about someone not getting what he wants, if this is the result of weighing his personal preferences against the personal preferences of others. But, if we take account of external preferences, the result will be that what some people get (more generally: how some people are affected by political decisions) will depend on what other people think of them. The black may end up with no car, *not* because his preferences lost out in the demand for cars, but because many racists did not want blacks to have cars. To take account of external preferences, Dworkin argues, is incompatible with the basic right to equal concern and respect on which the moral appeal of utilitarianism rests.

Dworkin's argument has not gone unquestioned, and the discussion has tended to focus on two issues. First there is the question of whether it is actually possible to distinguish between personal and external preferences. Suppose that our racist said that he did not want to *see* blacks driving cars, or even that he did not want to live in a society where blacks drove cars. These preferences could be said to relate to what *he* experiences, where *he* lives: does that make them personal preferences? Secondly, it is not entirely clear why taking account of external preferences should be thought incompatible with the basic right to equal concern and respect. Dworkin has suggested that taking account of external preferences involves a form of double counting. His point seems to be this. Suppose that people generally like blonds with blue eyes and want to see them prosper: they have an (external) preference that blonds should get whatever they want. Now suppose that you are a blond, and you would like a big shiny motor car. Your preference should be taken account of in calculating the general welfare. But, if we also take account of external preferences, your preference will be greatly re-inforced by the preferences of all those admirers of blonds. If you were a black in a society of racists, the effect of external preferences would be the reverse. The general point seems to be that a person is not being shown equal concern and respect if the importance attached to his interests, in the political process, is dependent on what people generally think of him.

But how does all this lead us to a theory of rights? Are we not now talking about a version of utilitarianism with external preferences excluded, rather than a theory of individual rights that trump considerations of utility? Dworkin's main idea is that external preferences cannot be excluded from the political process. The best we can do is to give special protection to those areas or aspects of conduct that are most likely to be affected by external preferences; and this protection should take the form of individual rights that override considerations of general welfare. Thus, we should recognise rights to free speech, because freedom of speech is very likely to be adversely affected by people's external preferences; the same is true, for example, of freedom of religion.

In Chapter 2 I suggested that Rawls has no very good reason for protecting, under his first principle, certain liberties and not others. Such discrimination between liberties, I argued, could only be justified by some conception of what liberties were important for the sort of life people *ought* to lead: thus we might prefer freedom of religion to freedom of property. But this kind of discrimination should not be open to Rawls, who purports to offer a theory that is neutral between different conceptions of the good life. Modern liberals such as Rawls emphasise the importance of "civil liberties" such as freedom of speech. They are much less concerned about (often they are positively hostile to) the "market liberties" of freedom of contract and property. Is this simply an arbitrary prejudice on their part?

We can now see that Dworkin's theory offers an alternative approach to this problem, via the exclusion of external preferences. Freedom of speech and freedom of religion are likely to be the subject of external preferences, and therefore merit special protection. Freedom of contract and of property are far less likely to suffer from the problem of external preferences: restrictions on the power to dispose of property, and on the terms that may be introduced into consumer agreements or contracts of employment, are likely to be imposed in order to maximise the fulfillment of personal preferences. There are, on this argument, good reasons for protecting the traditional "civil liberties" in a way that the "market liberties" are not protected.

151

SELECTED READING

JOHN GRAY, "Indirect Utility and Fundamental Rights" in E. F. PAUL, J. PAUL, and F. D. MILLER (Eds.), *Human Rights* (1984).

H. L. A. HART, *Essays in Jurisprudence and Philosophy* (1983), Essays 8 and 9.

H. L. A. HART, *Essays on Bentham* (1982).

T. M. SCANLON, "Rights, Goals and Fairness" in J. WALDRON (Ed.), *Theories of Rights* (1984).

DAVID LYONS "Utility and Rights" in J. WALDRON, *op. cit.*

H. L. A. HART "Are There any Natural Rights?" (1955) *Philosophical Review* 175 (also in J. WALDRON, *op. cit.*).

T. M. BENDITT, *Rights* (1982).

RONALD DWORKIN, *Taking Rights Seriously* (1978) Chaps. 7 and 12 (see also Dworkin's ?essay in J. WALDRON, *op. cit.*).

Index

153